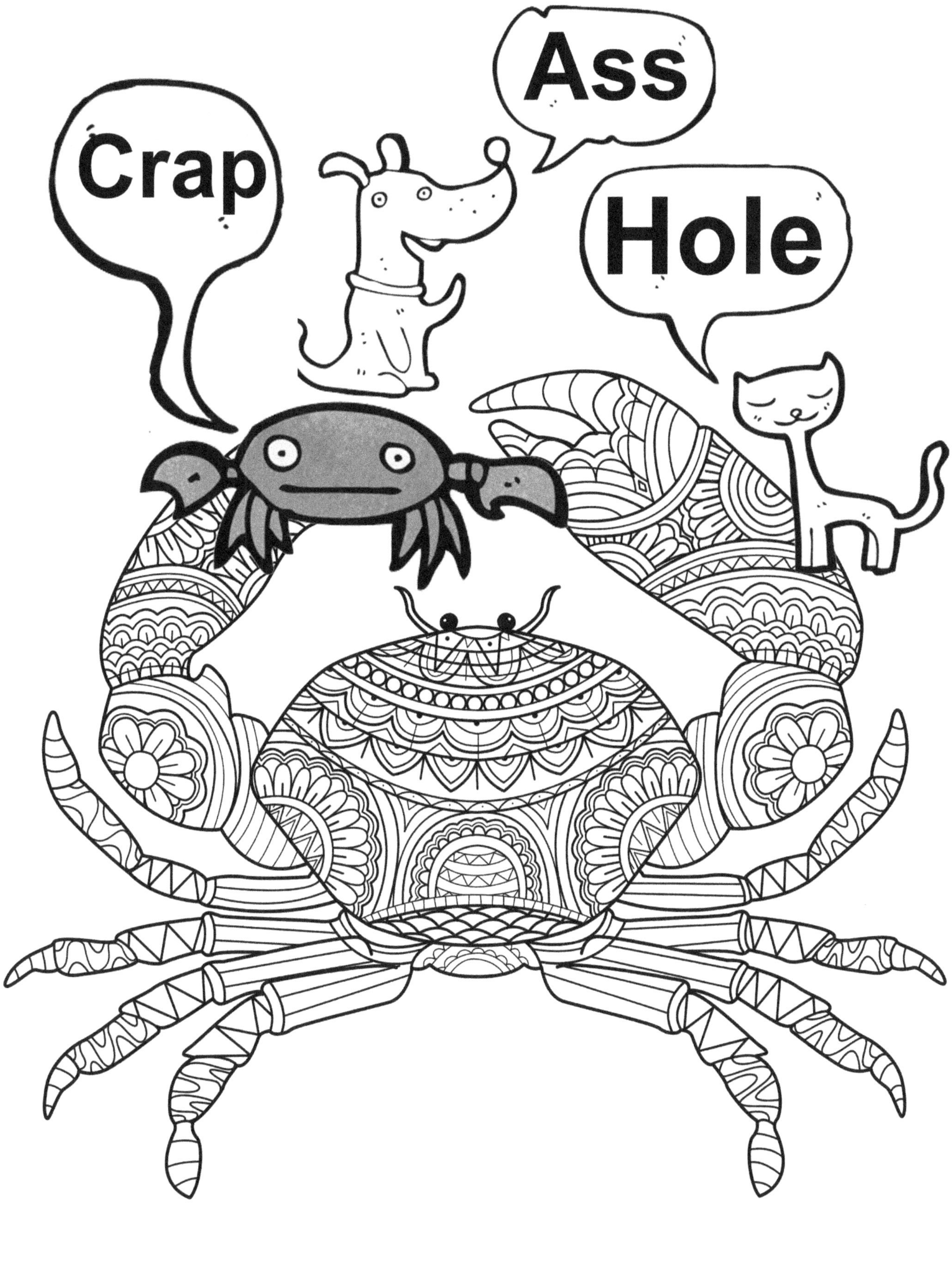

I0462390

Illustrated by:
Mandala & Caricature Illustration
Joshua Lazana Lagman and Jade Villaremo

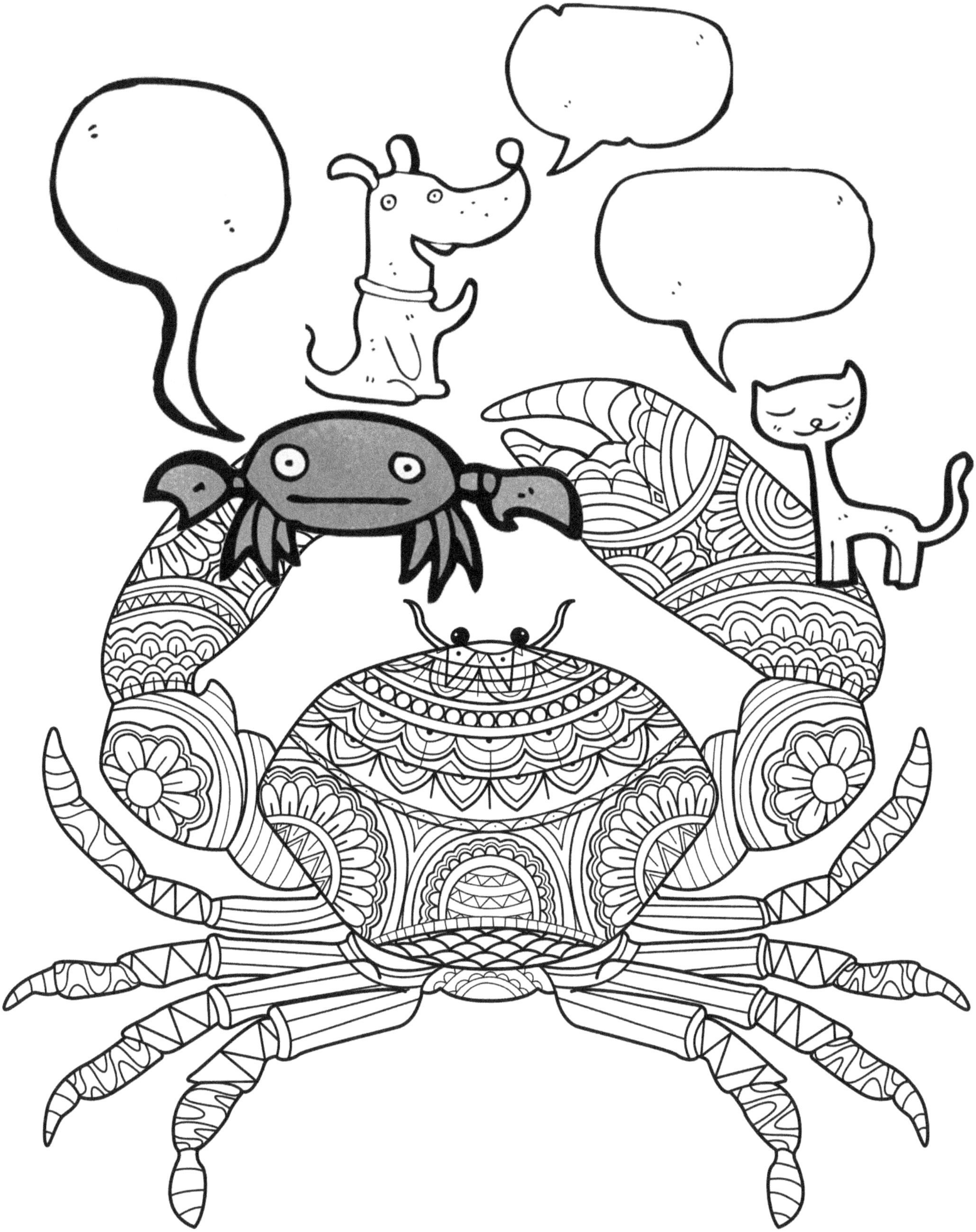

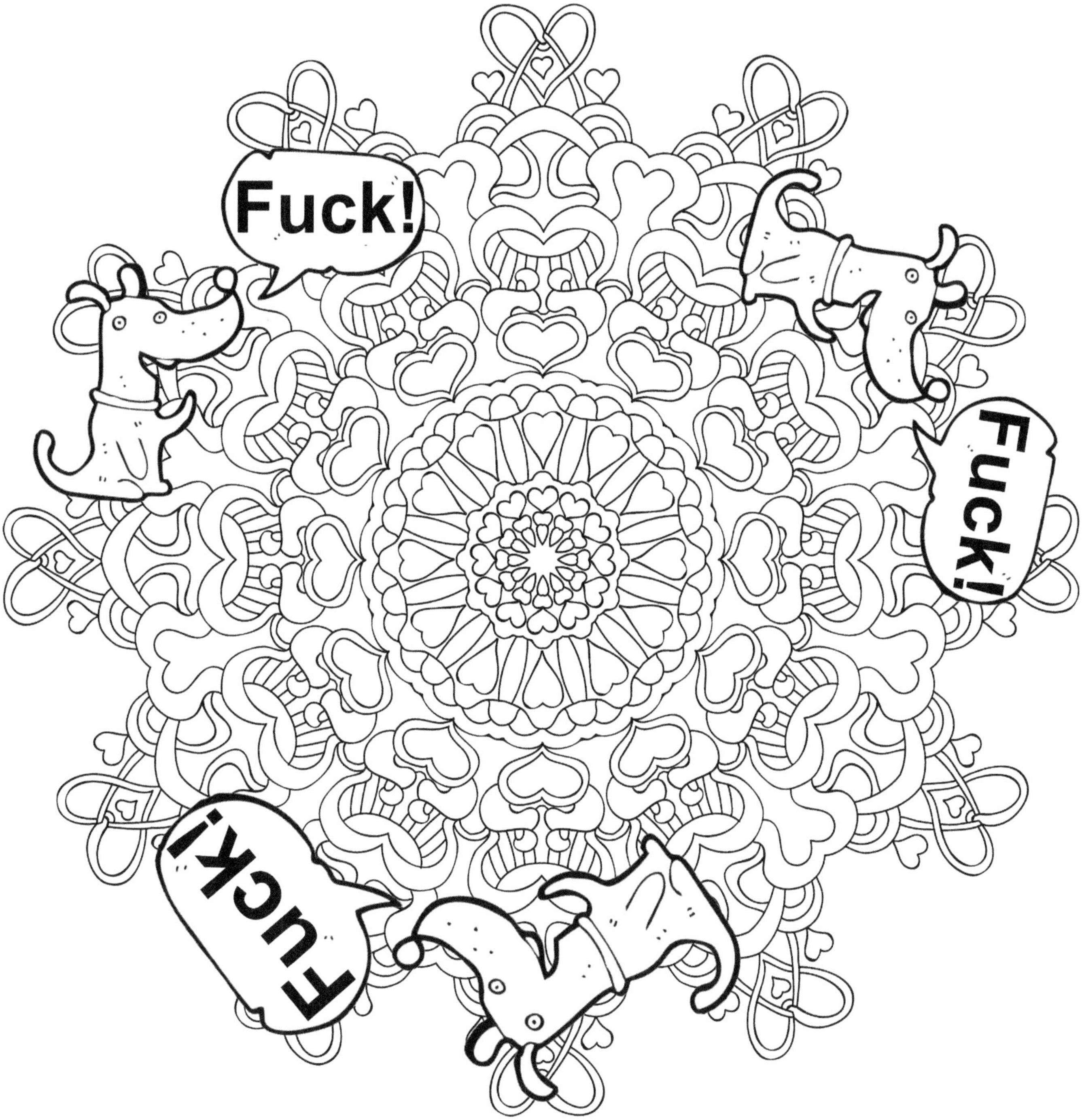
Fuck!
Fuck!
Fuck!

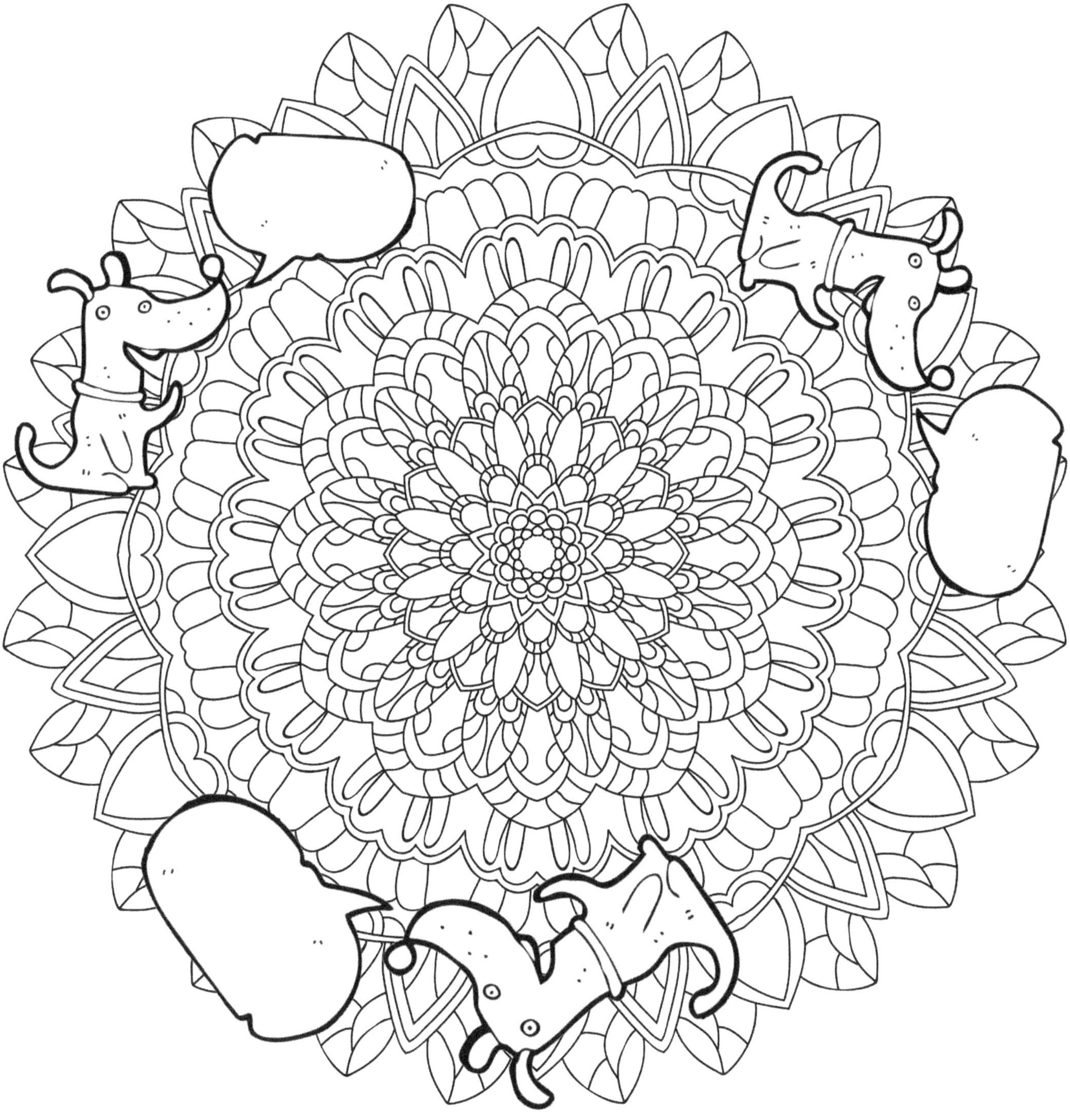

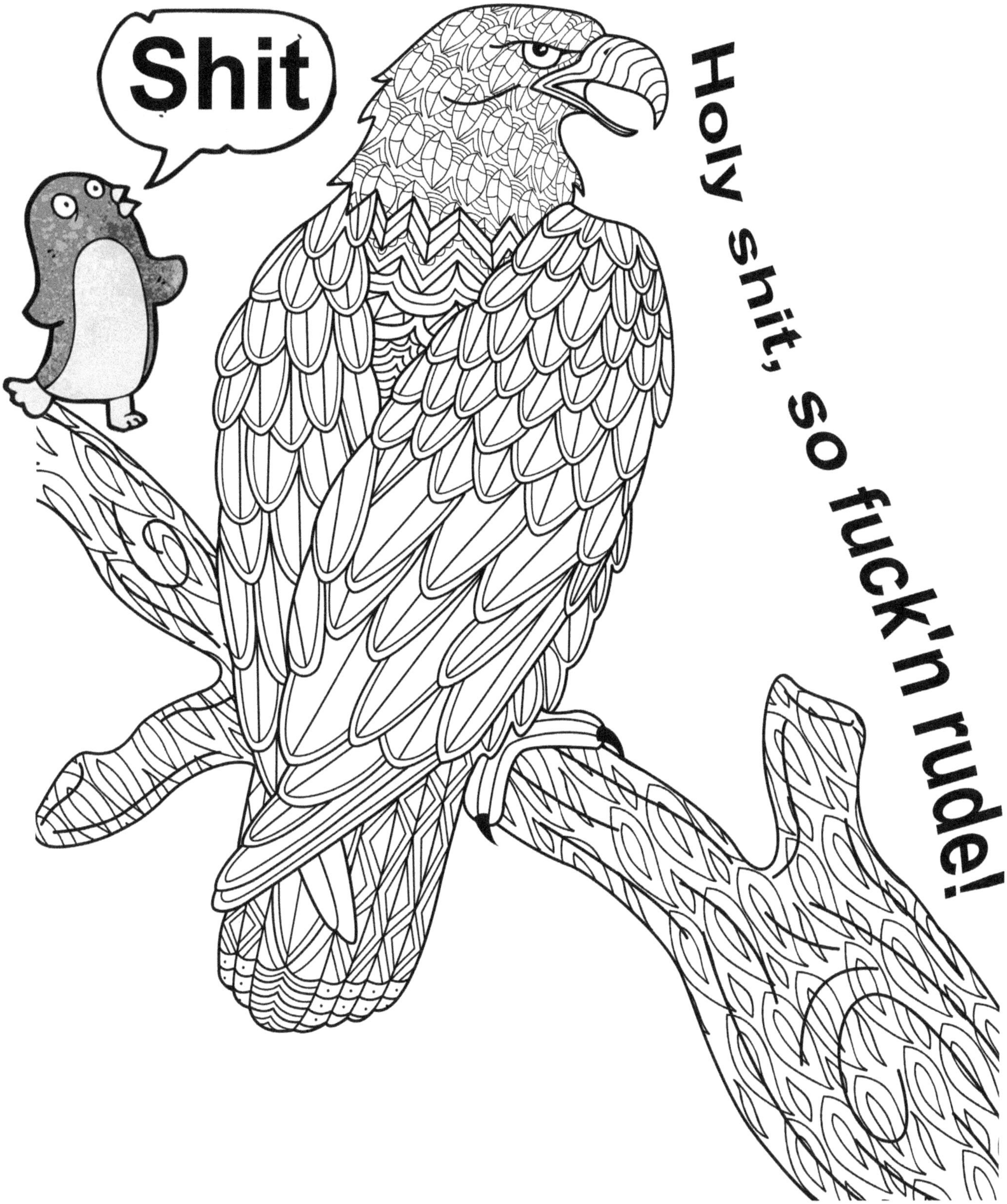
Shit
Holy shit, so fuck'n rude!

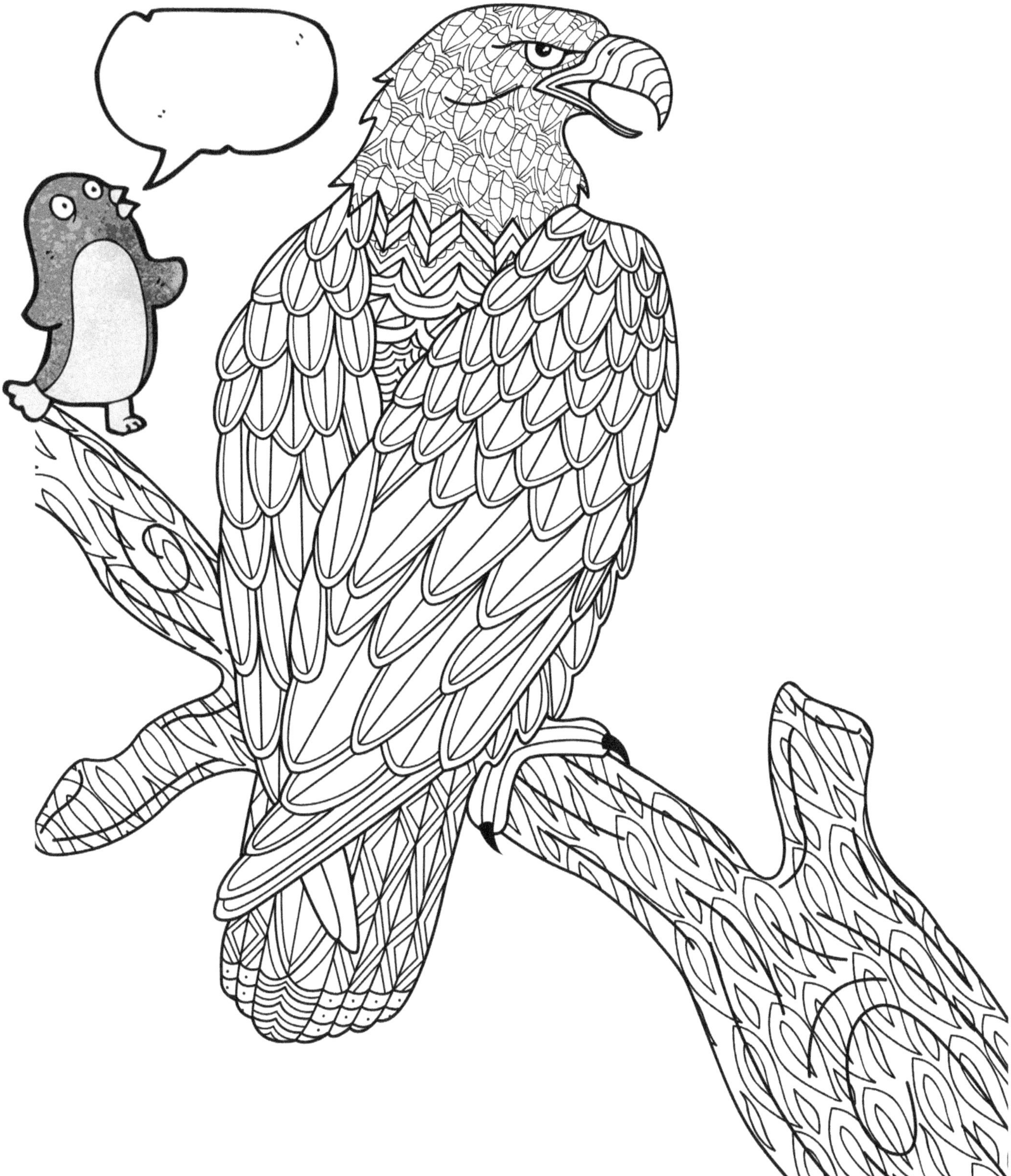

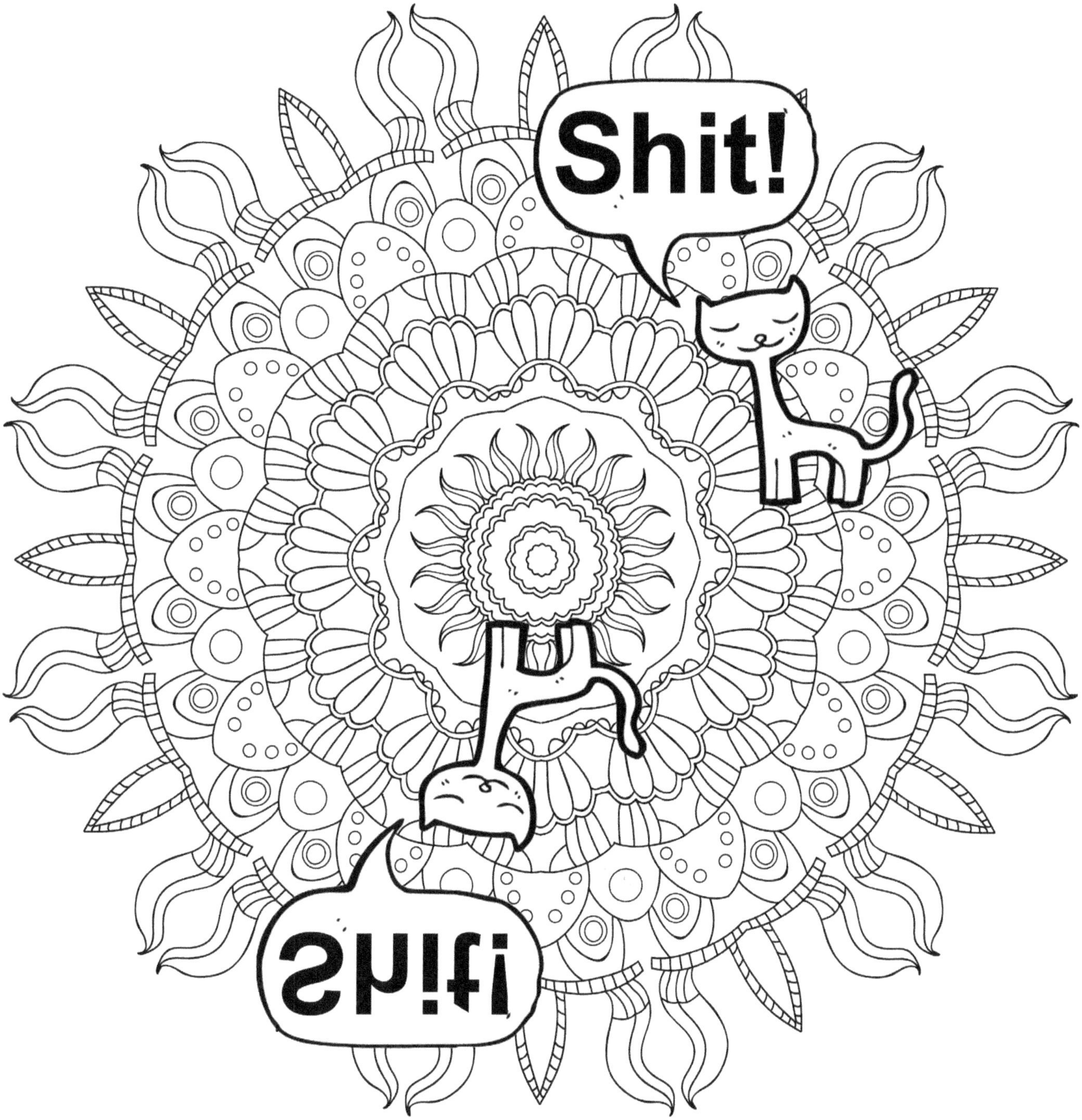
Shit!
Shit!

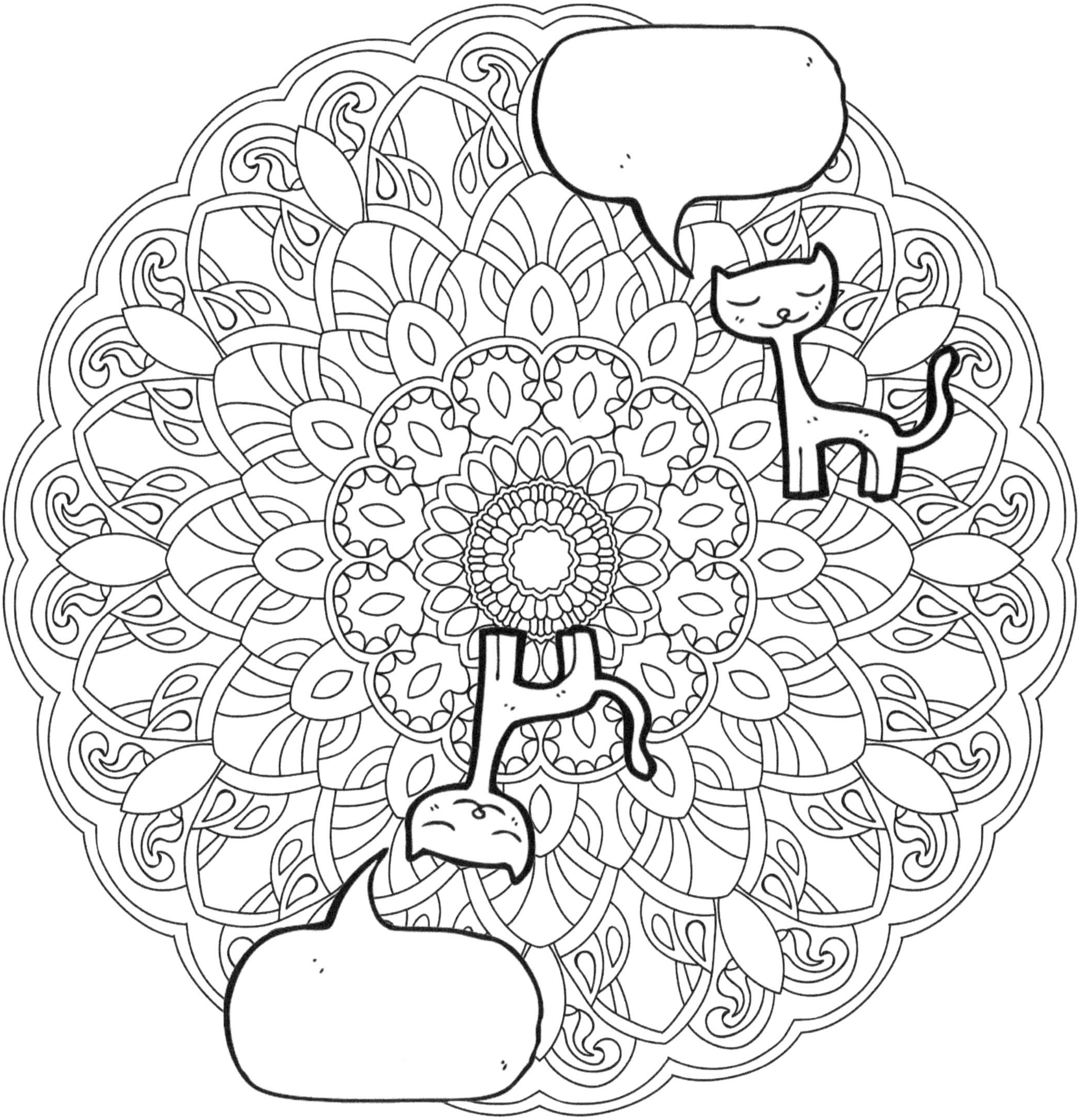

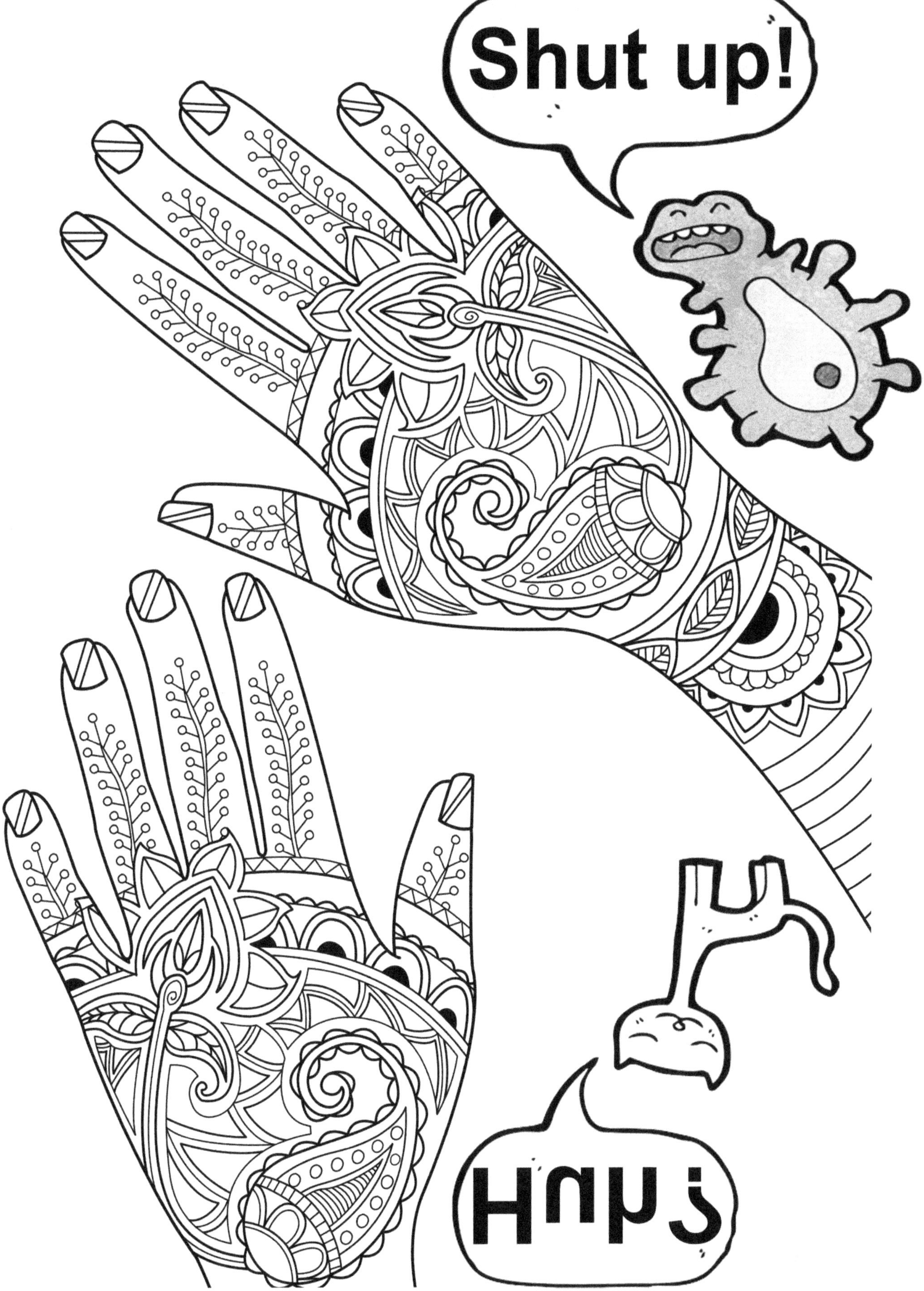
Shut up!

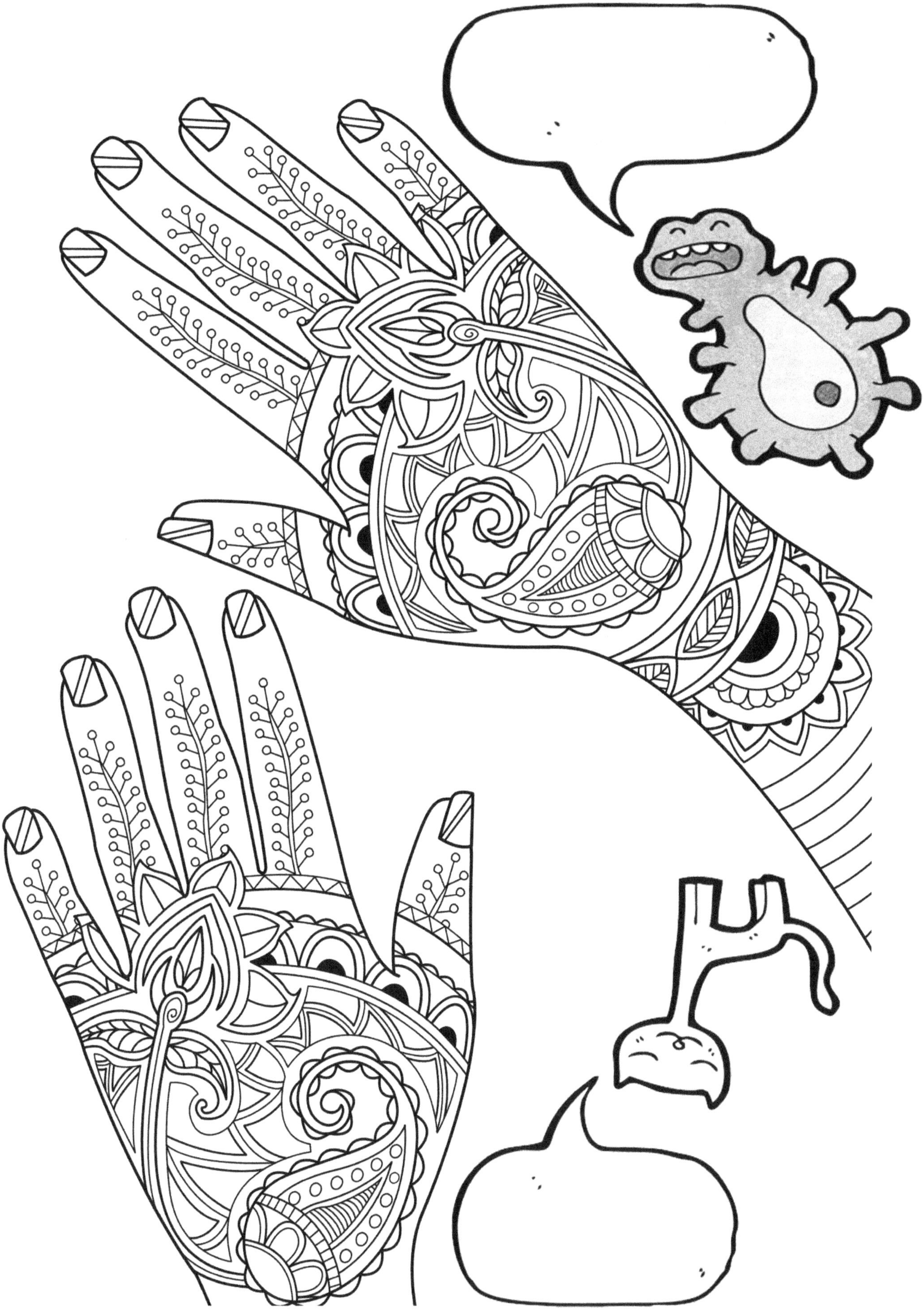

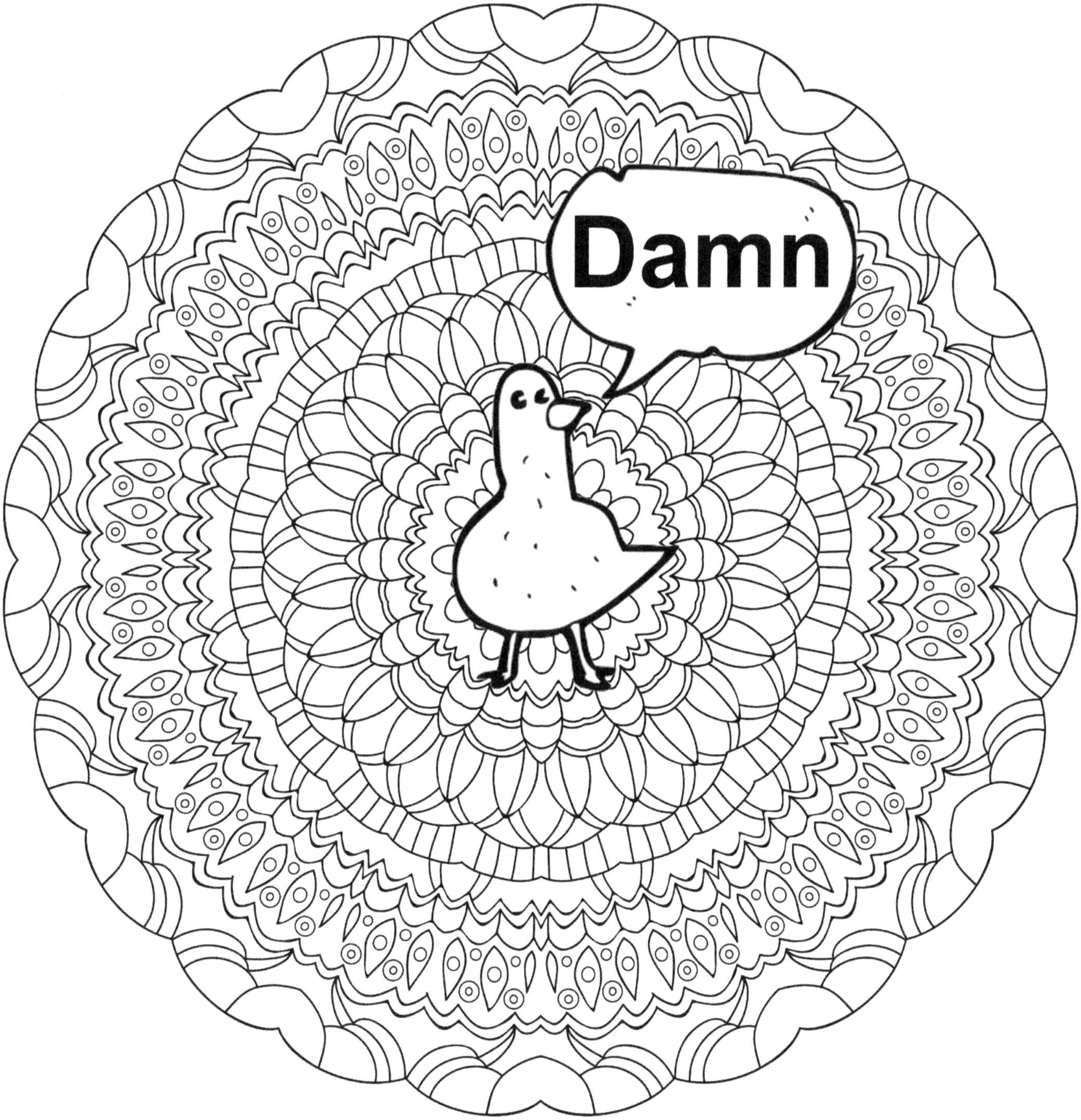
Damn

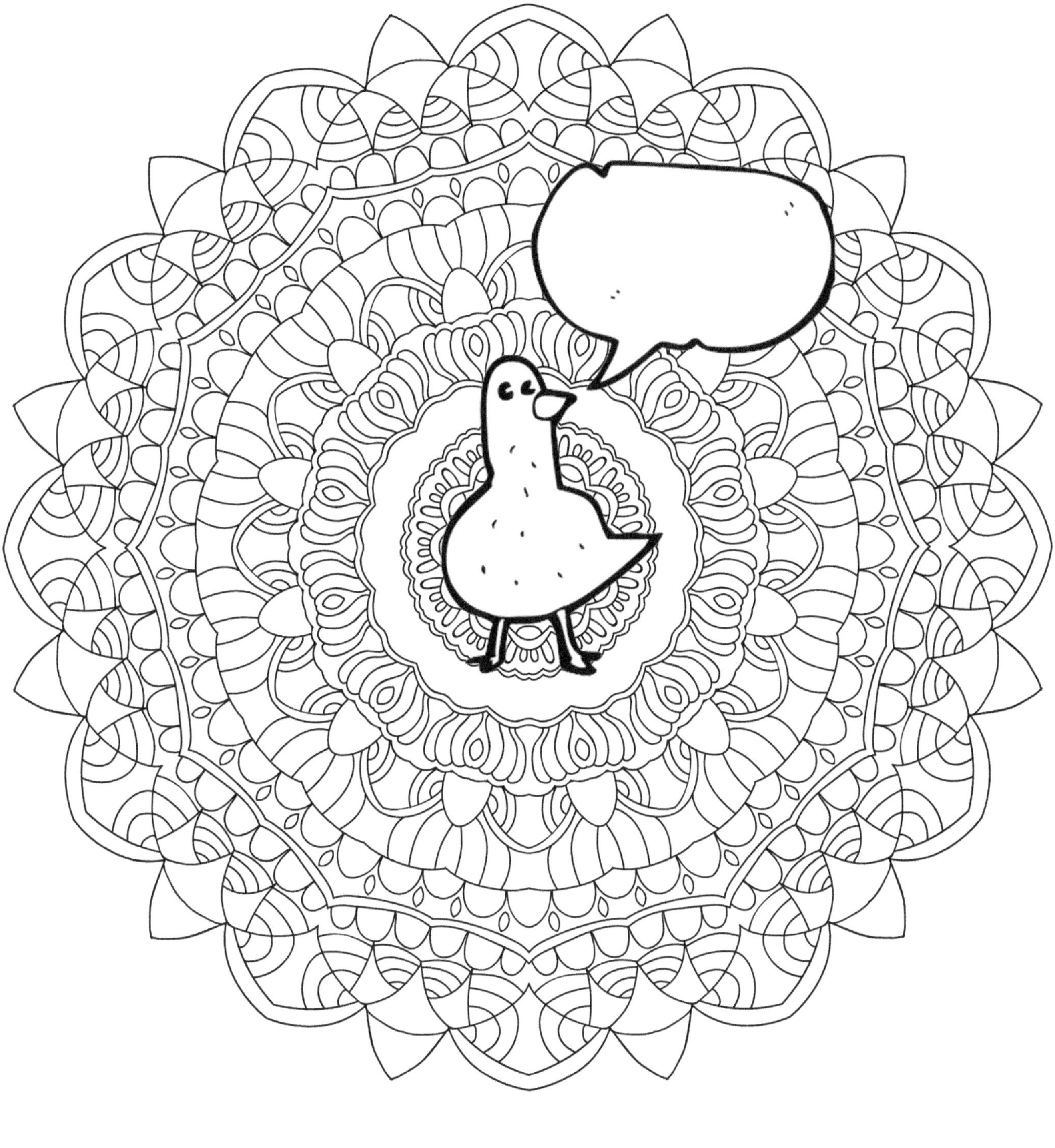

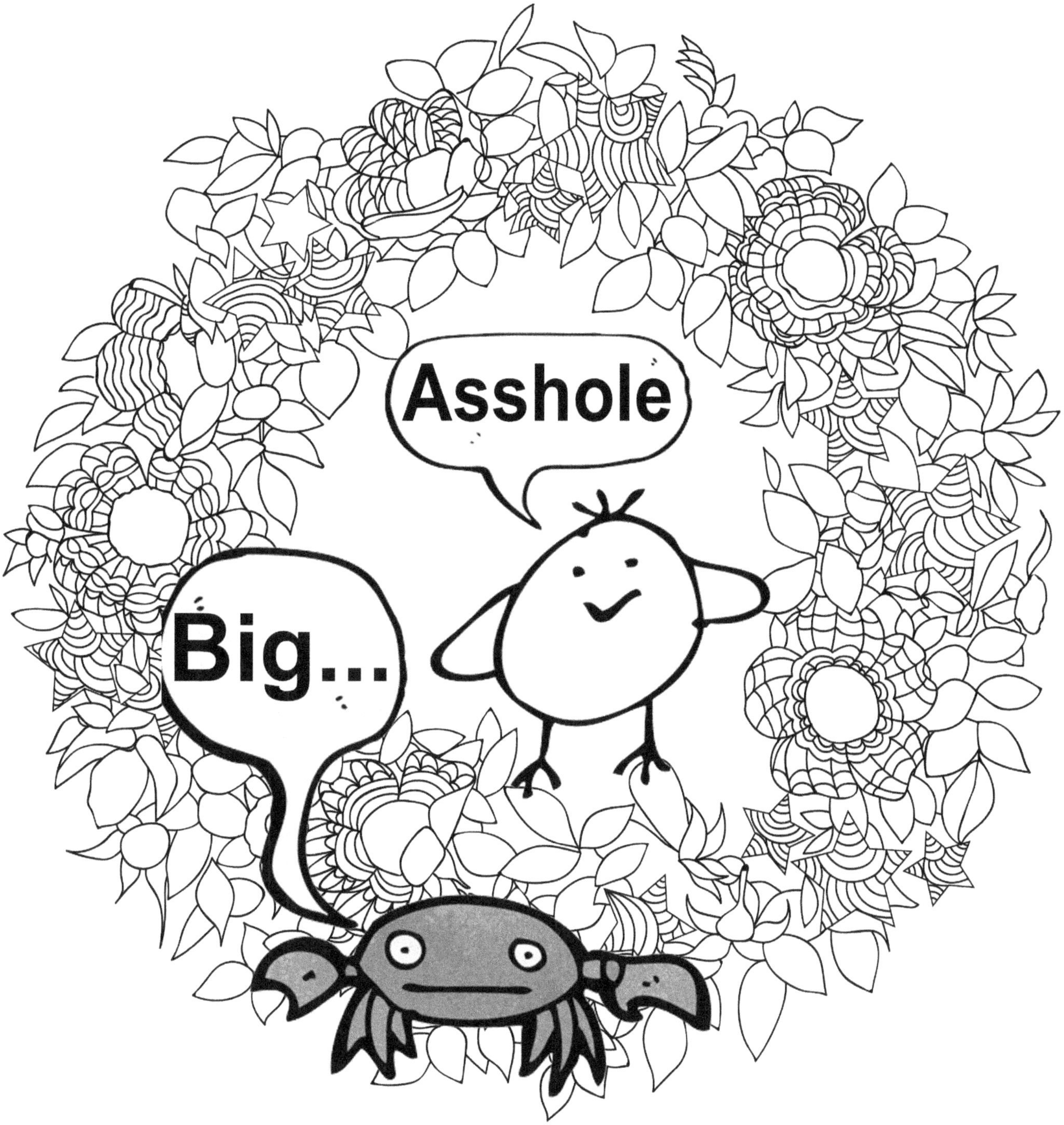
Asshole
Big...

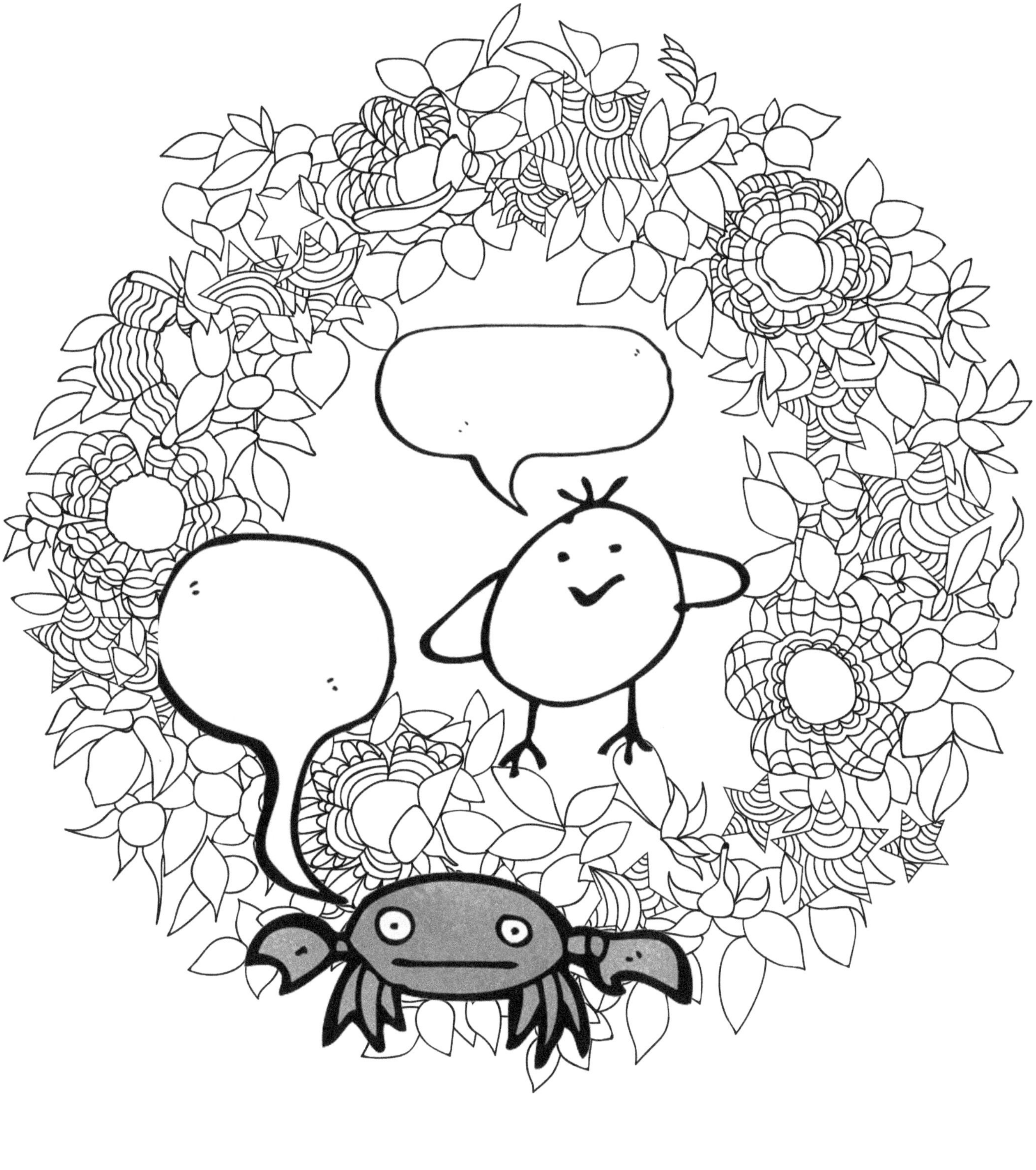

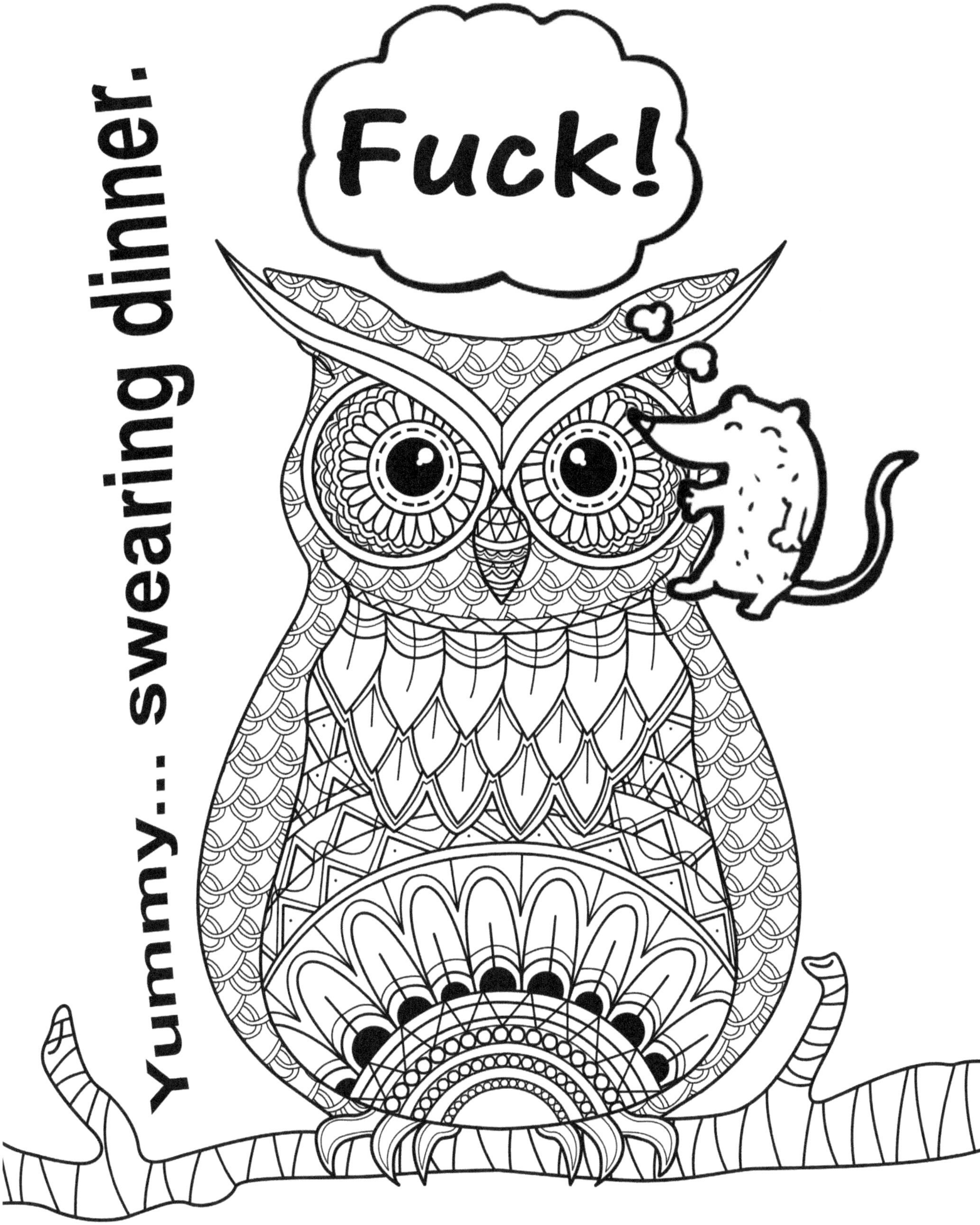
Fuck!
Yummy... swearing dinner.

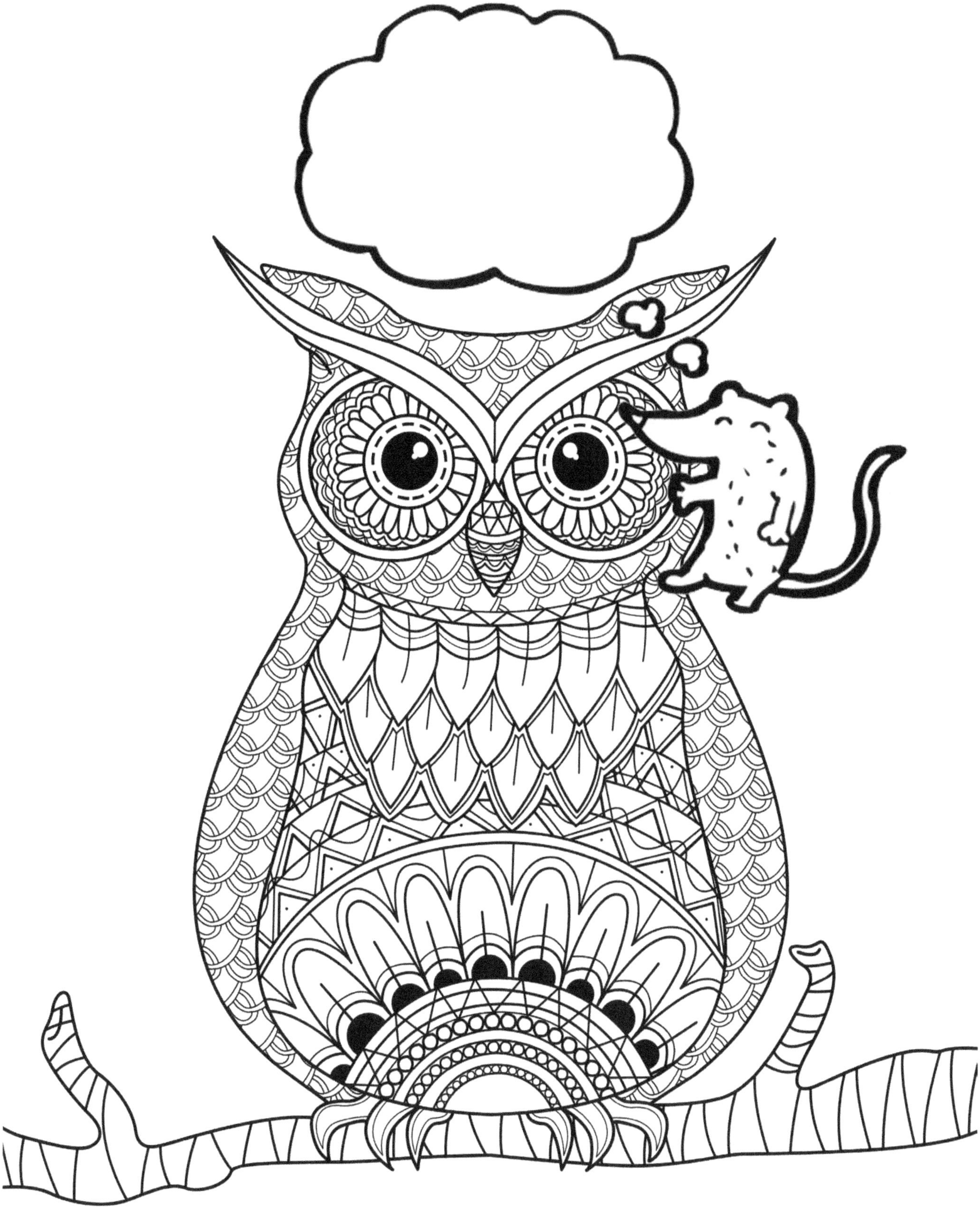

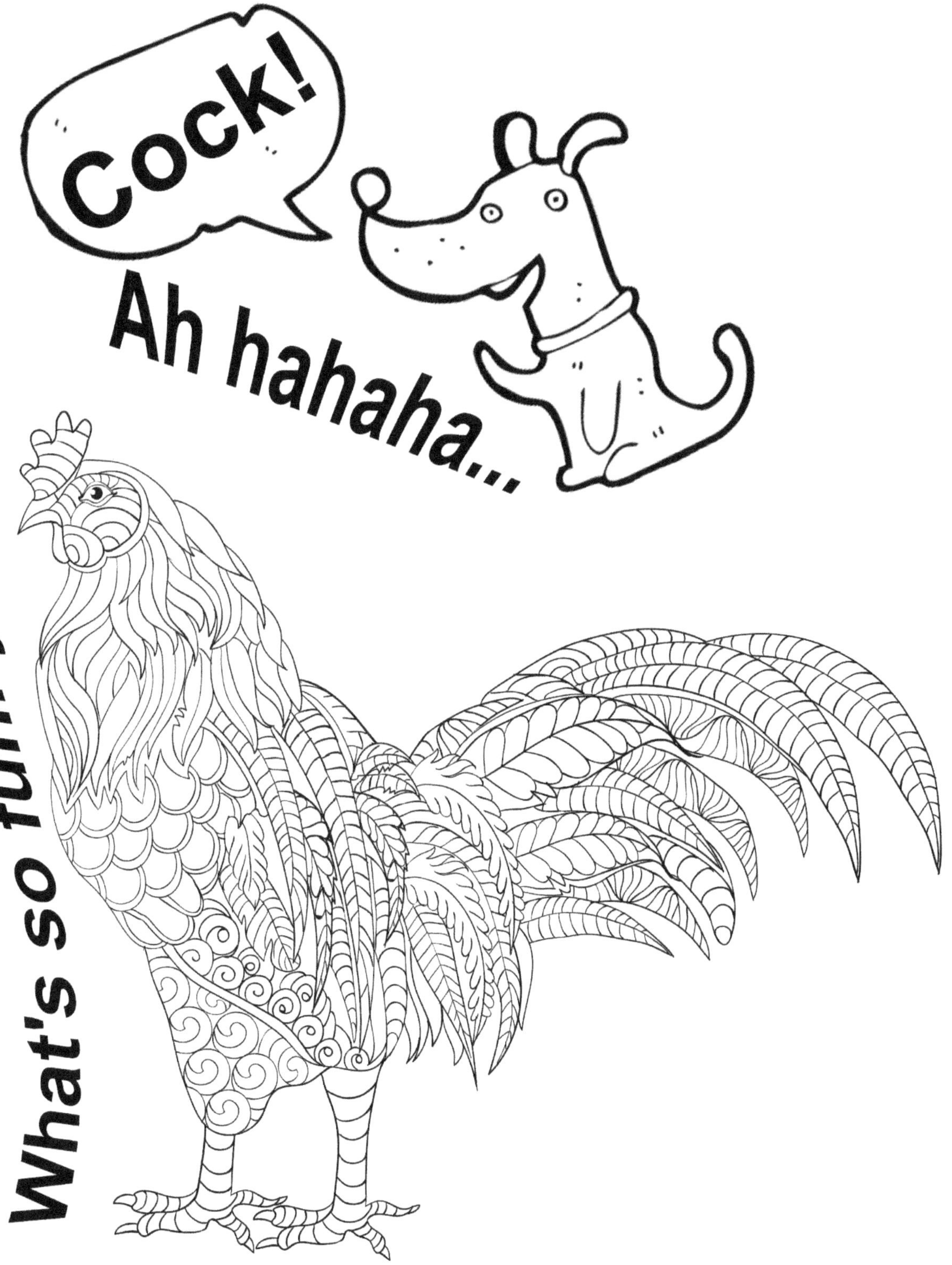
Cock!
Ah hahaha...
What's so funny? You fat ass!

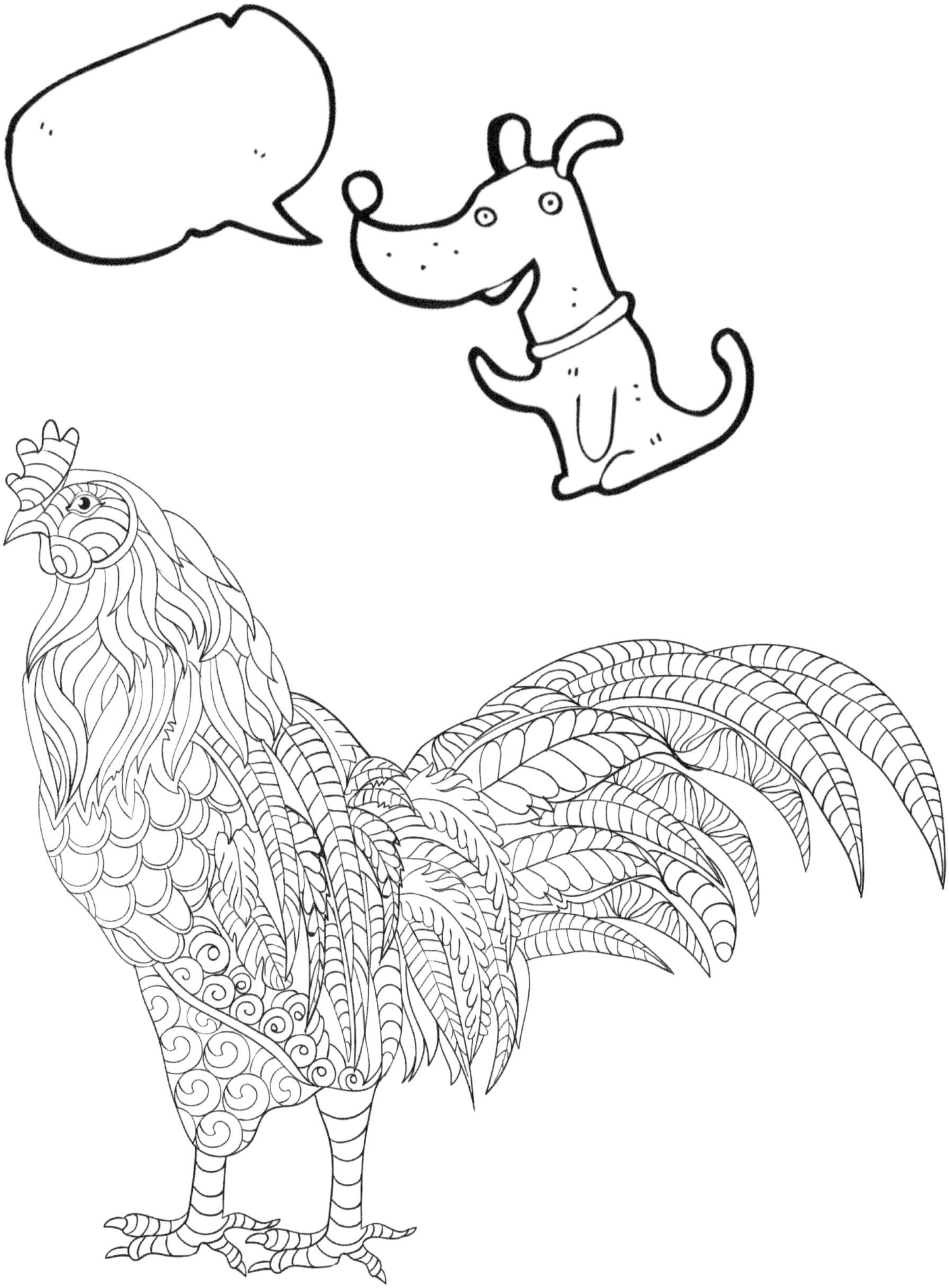

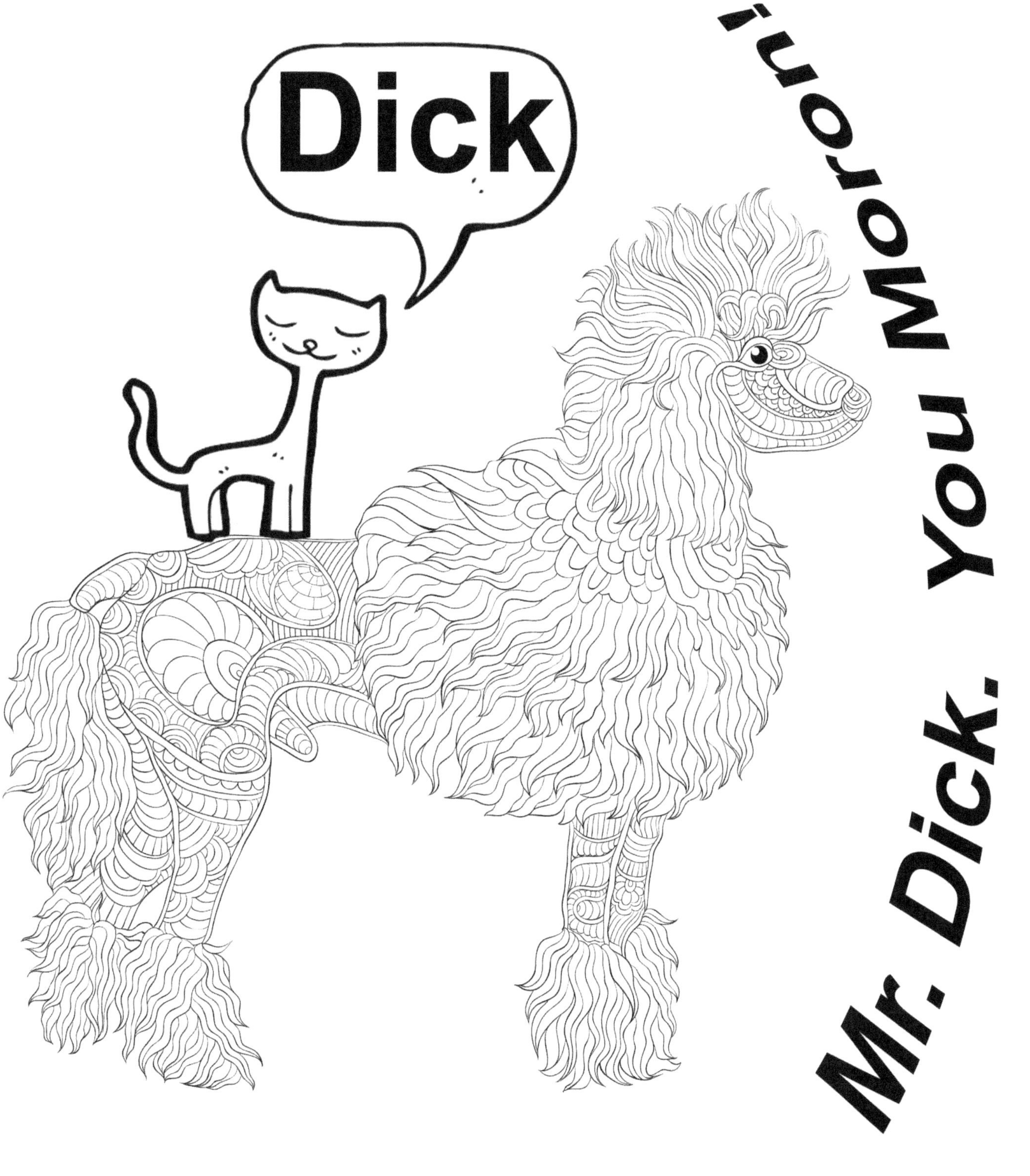
Dick
Mr. Dick. You Moron!

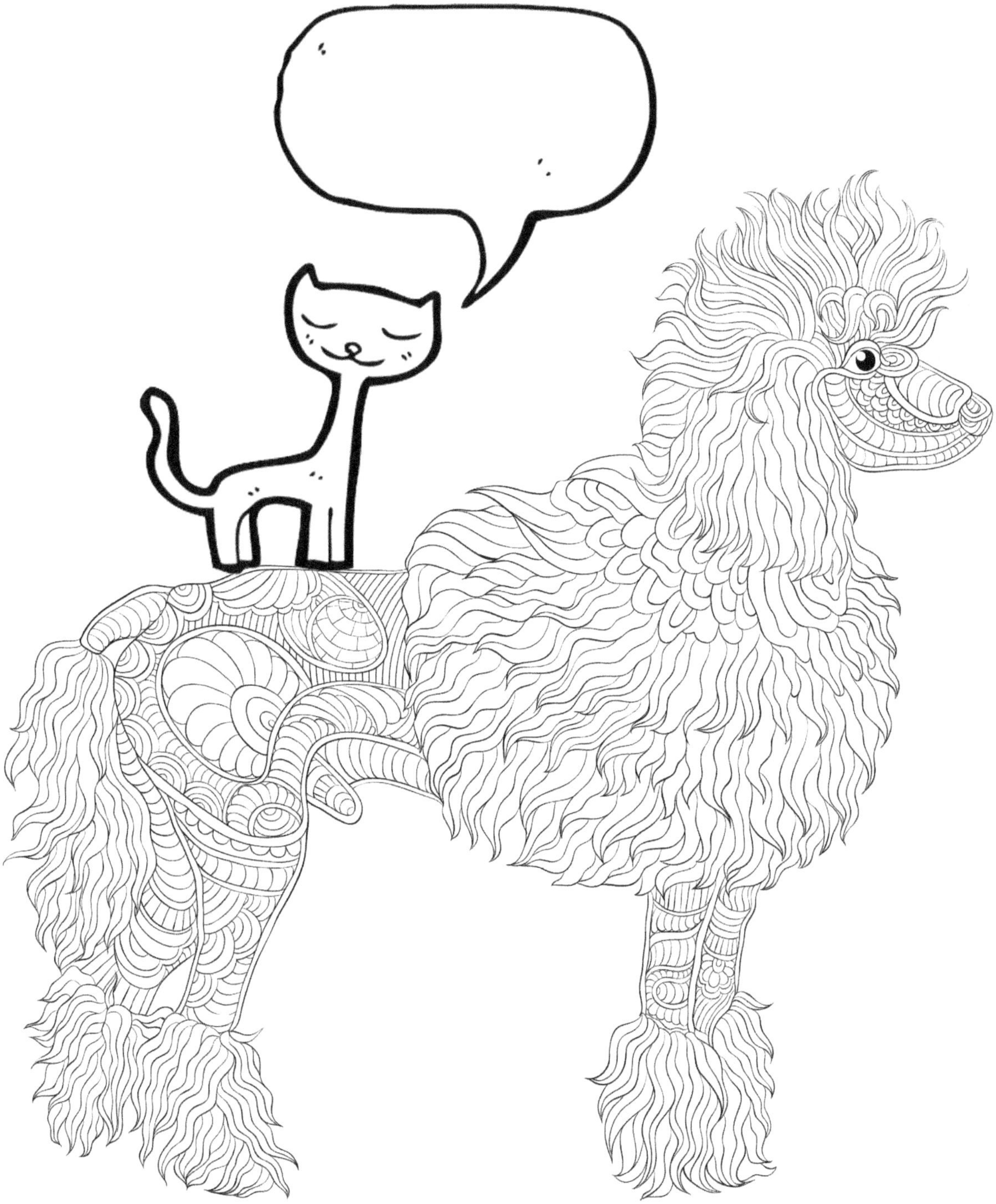

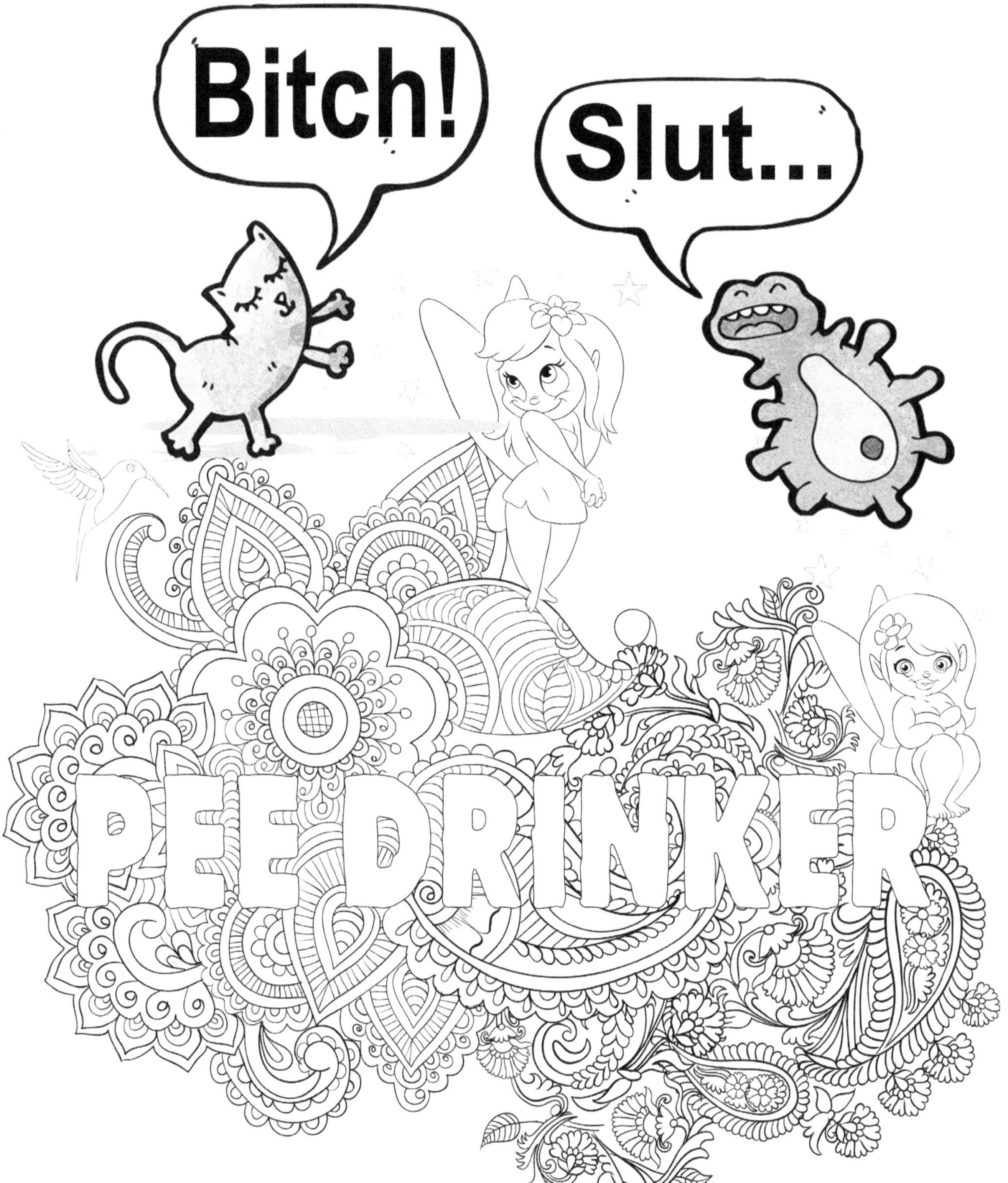
Bitch!
Slut...
PEE DRINKER

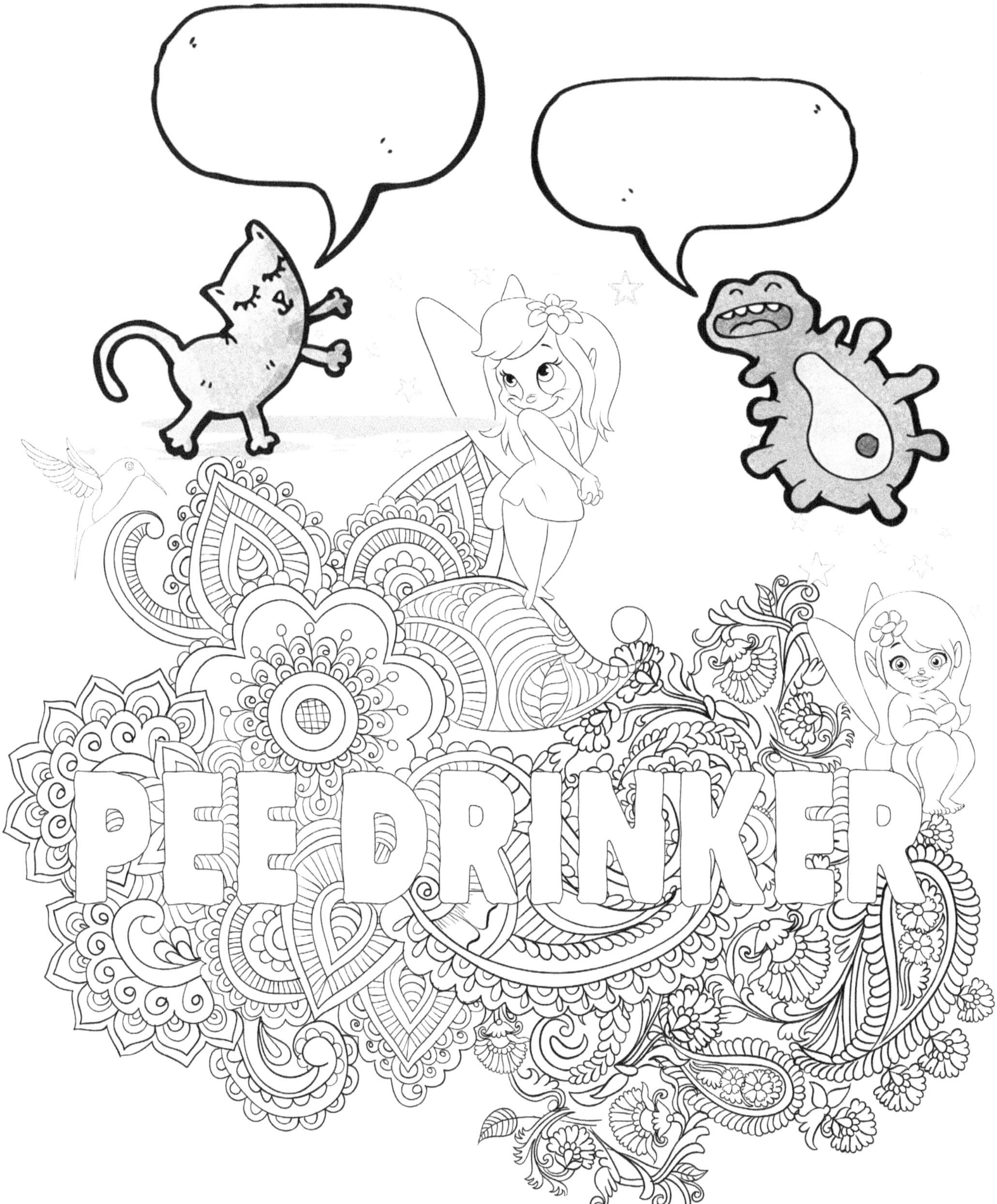
PEE DRINKER

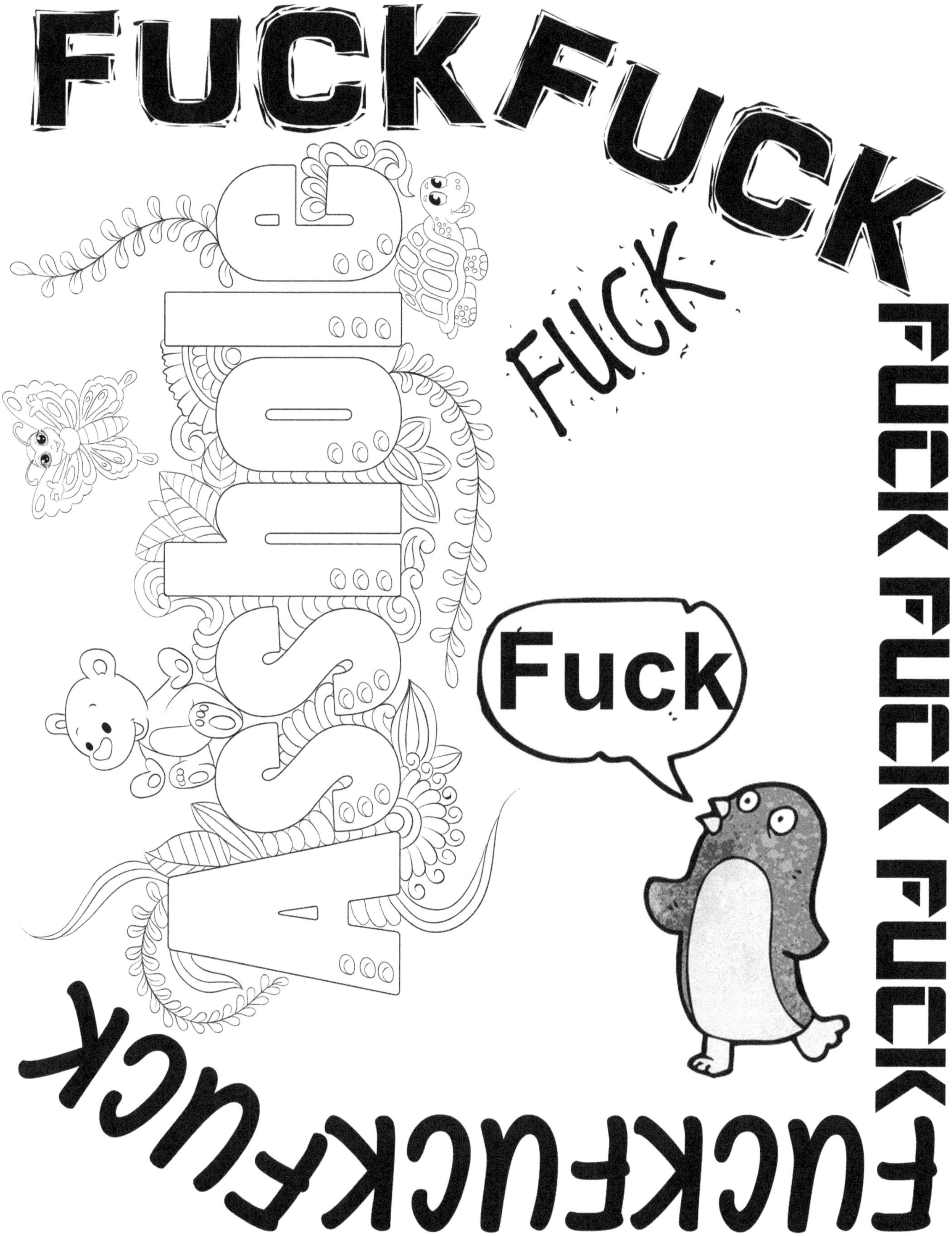
FUCK FUCK
FUCK
Asshole
Fuck
FUCK FUCK FUCK FUCK
FUCKFUCKFUCK

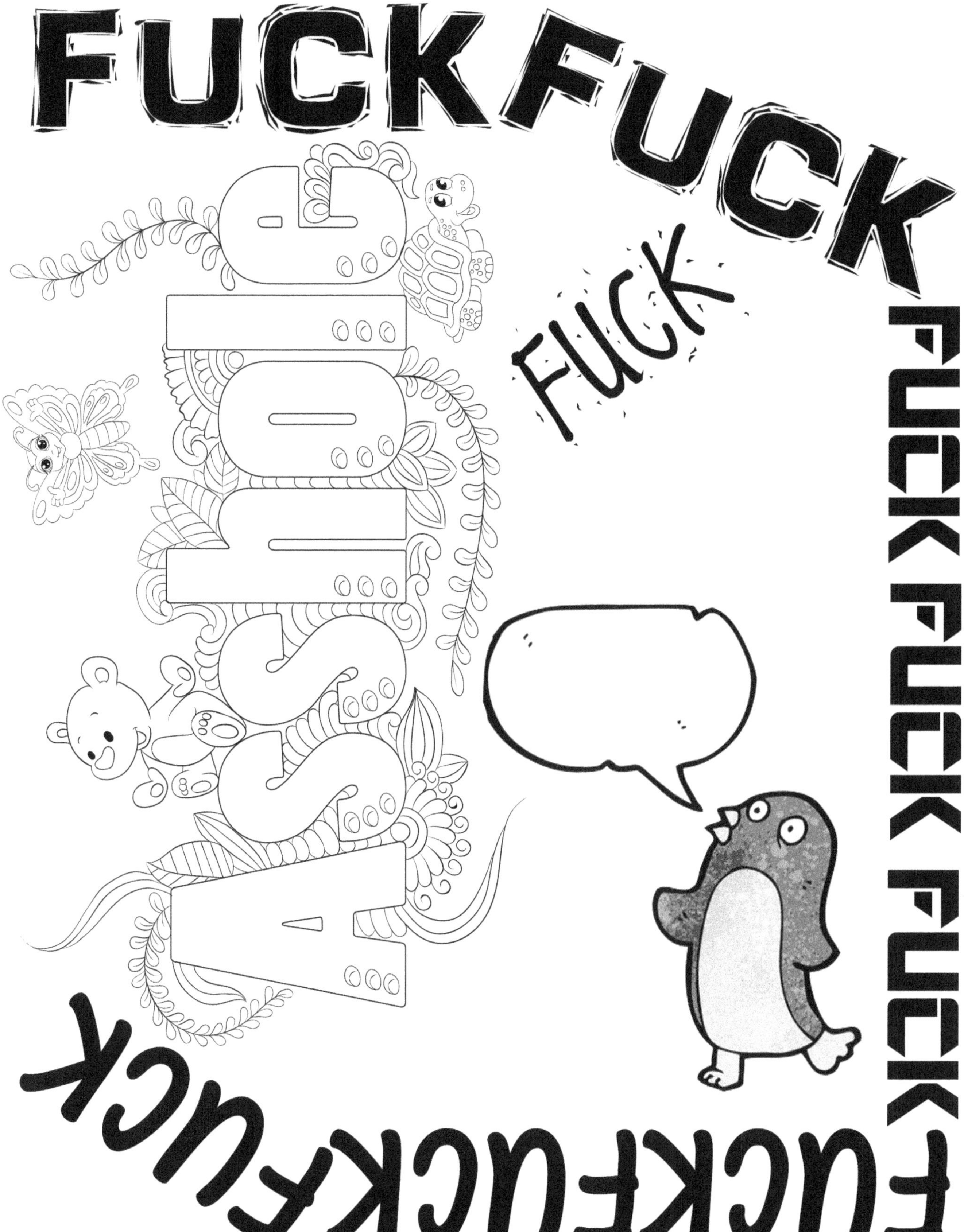
FUCK FUCK
FUCK
Asshole
FUCK FUCK FUCK FUCK
FUCKFUCKFUCK

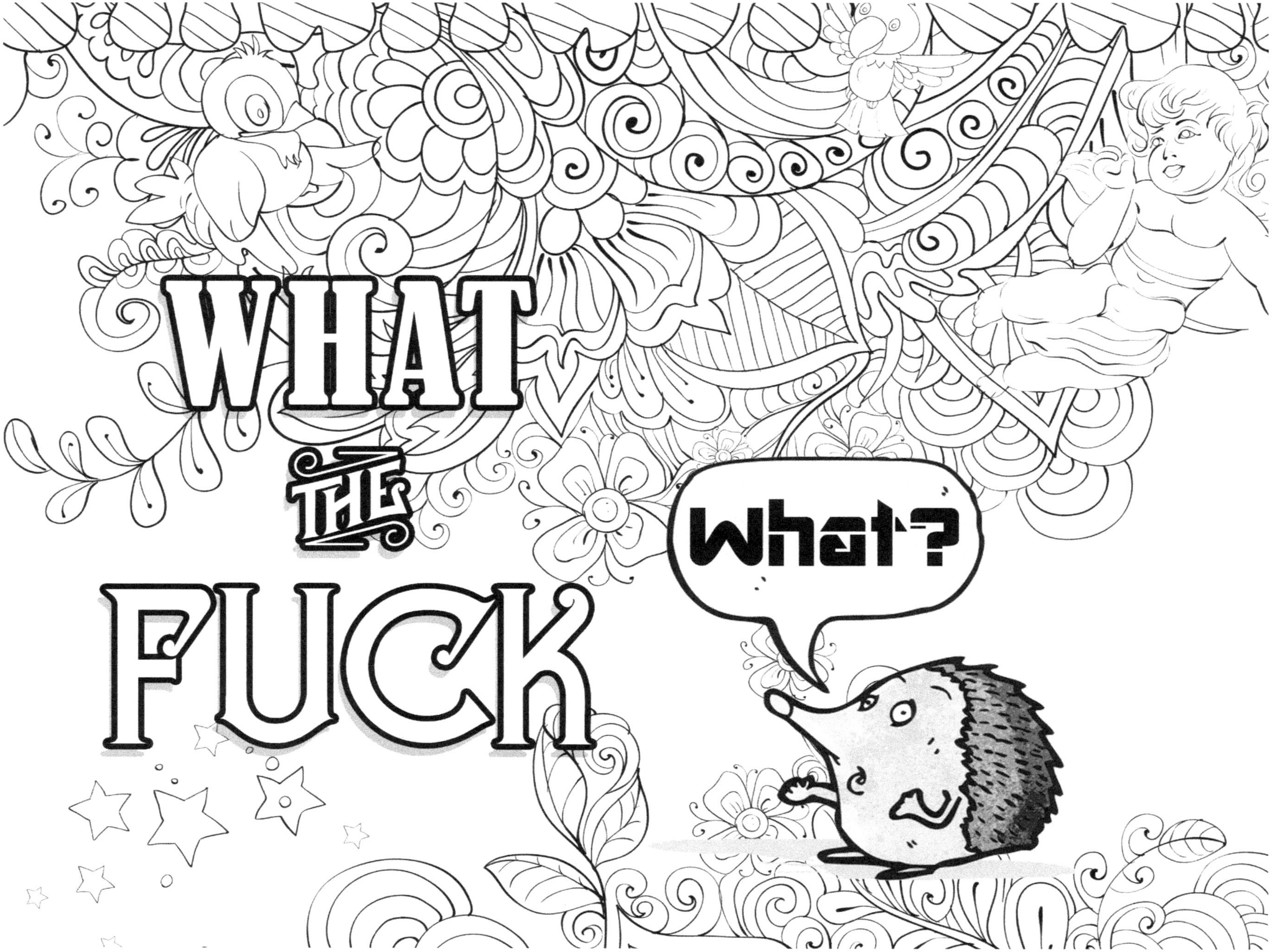
WHAT THE FUCK
What?

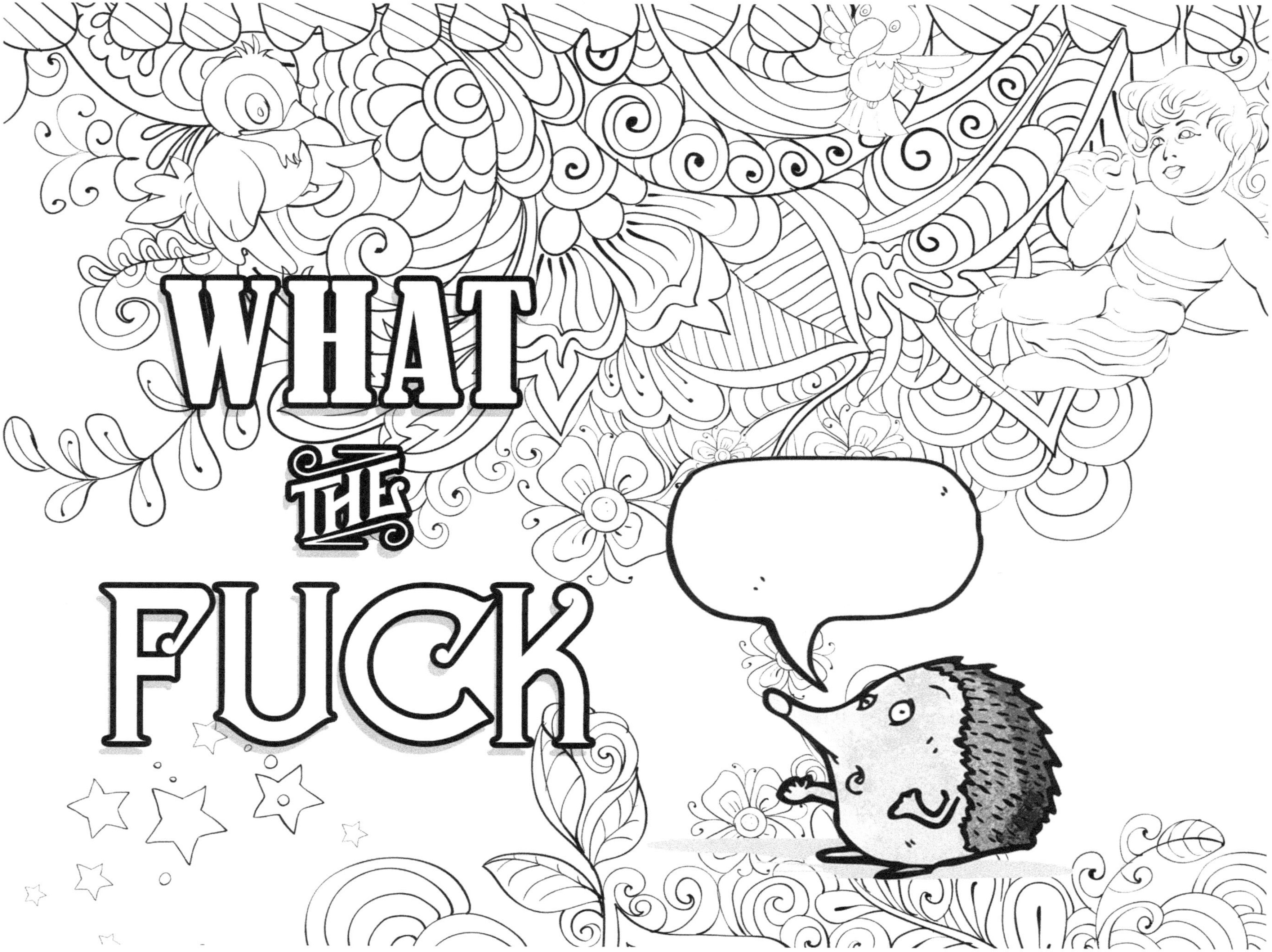
WHAT
THE
FUCK

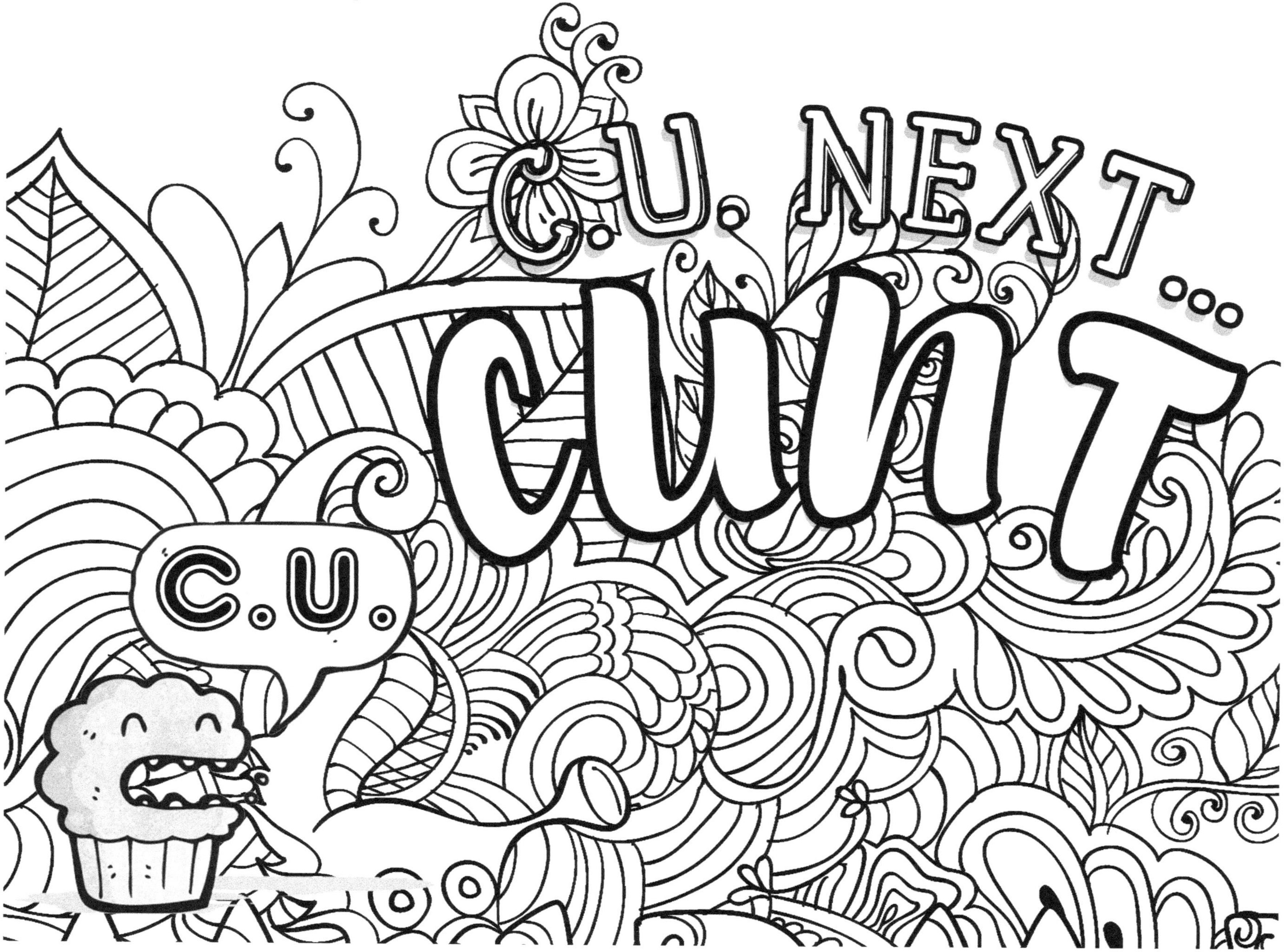
C.U. NEXT ...
CUNT
C.U.

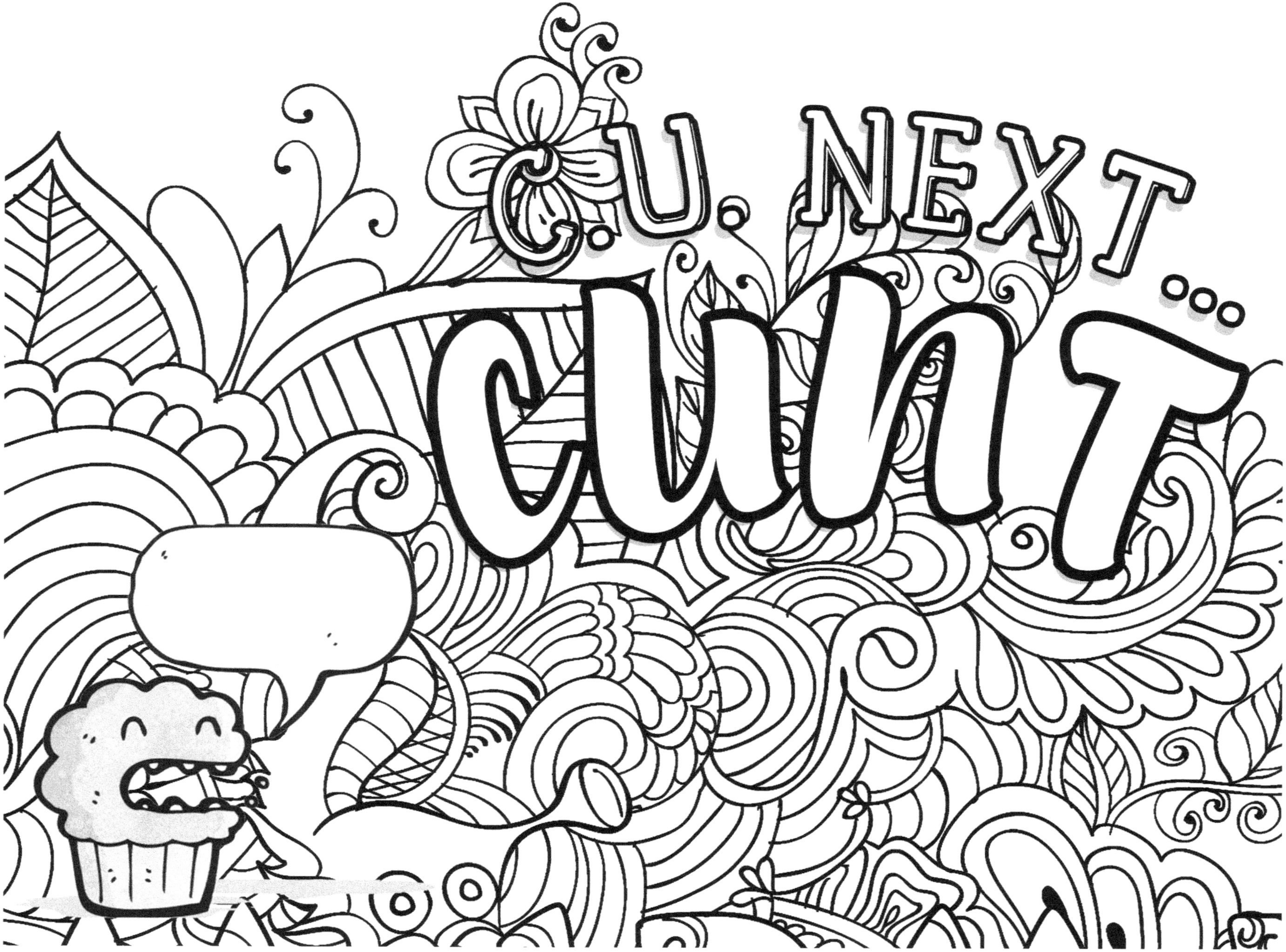
C.U. NEXT ...
CUNT

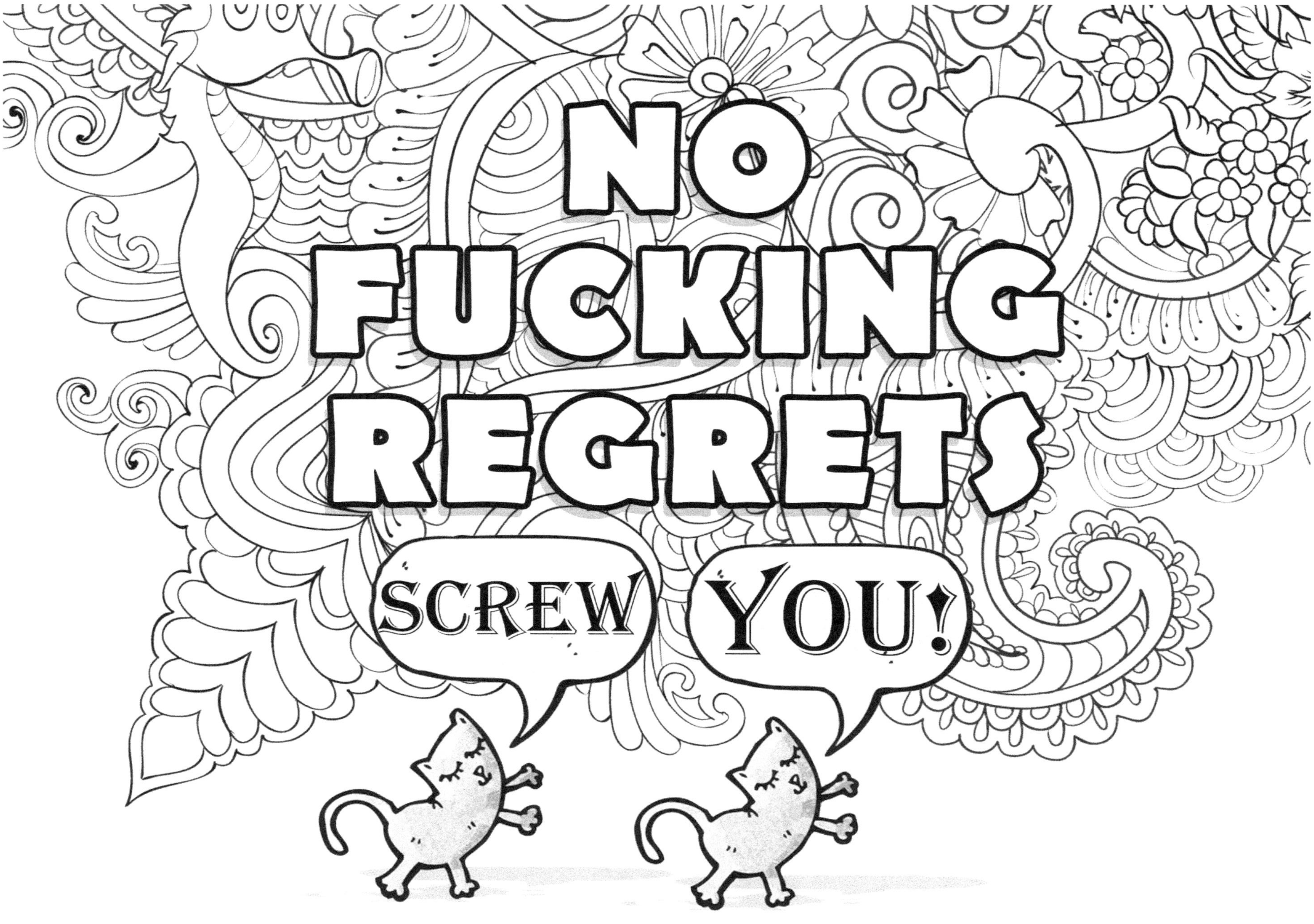
NO FUCKING REGRETS
SCREW
YOU!

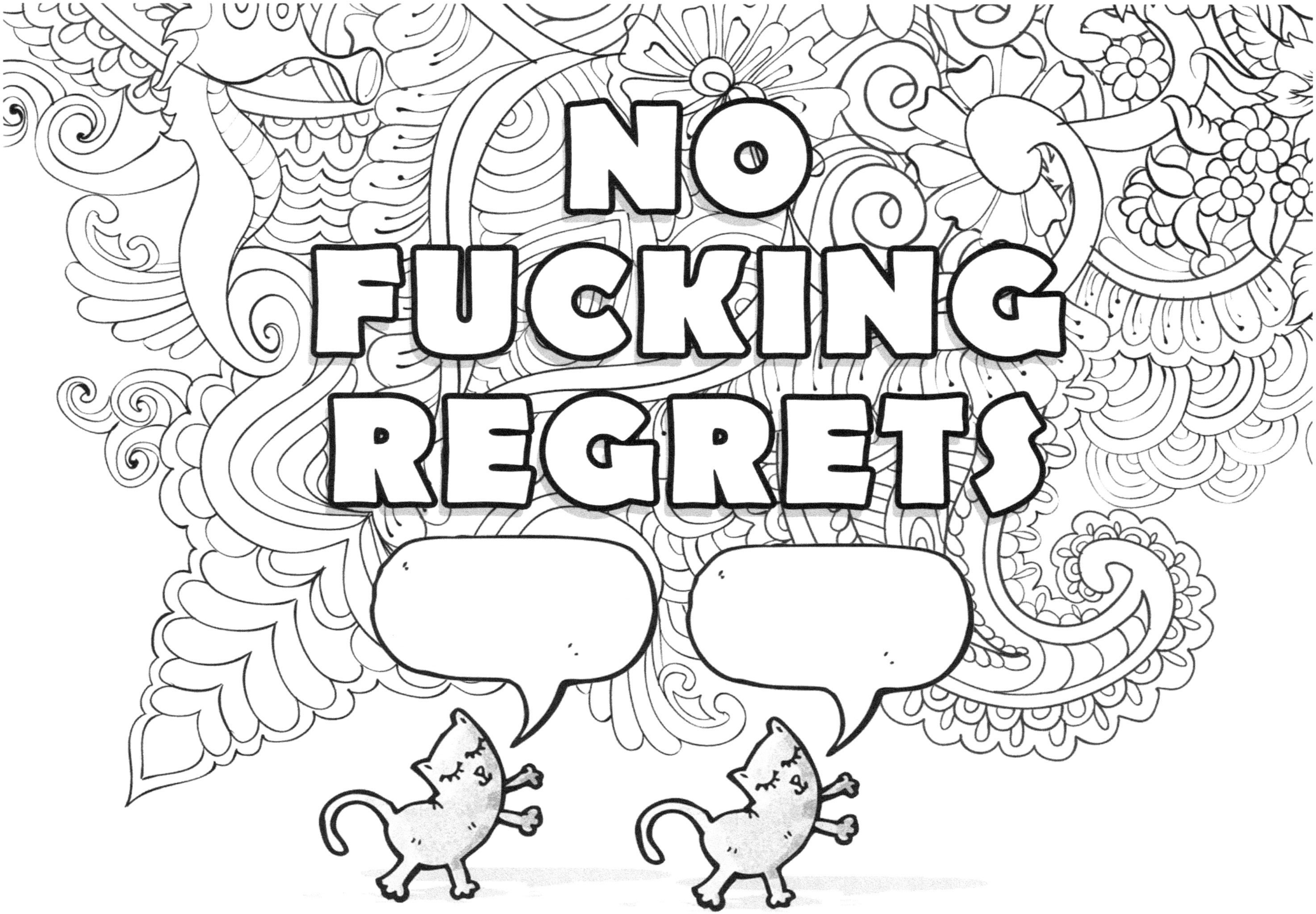
NO
FUCKING
REGRETS

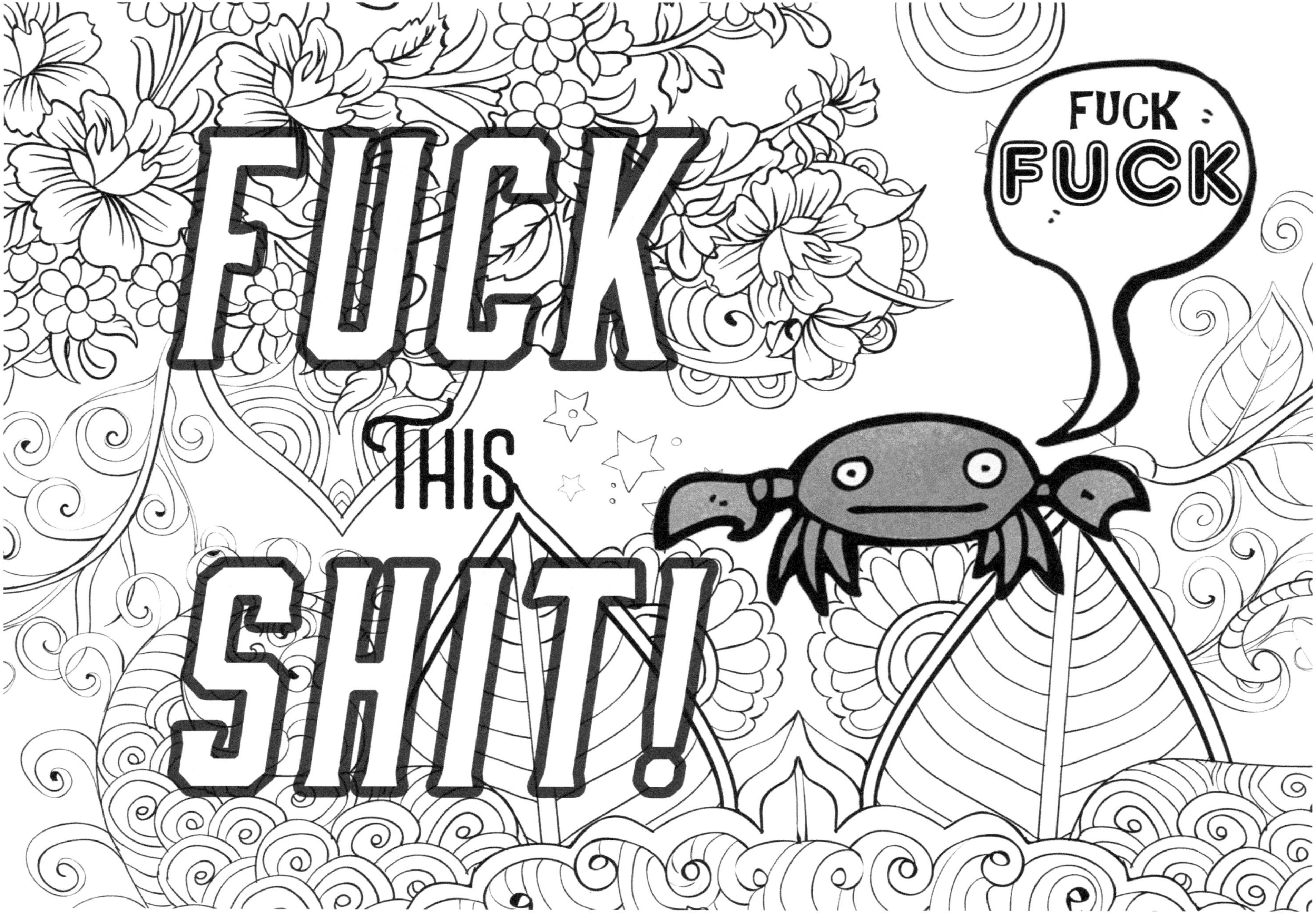
FUCK
THIS
SHIT!
FUCK FUCK

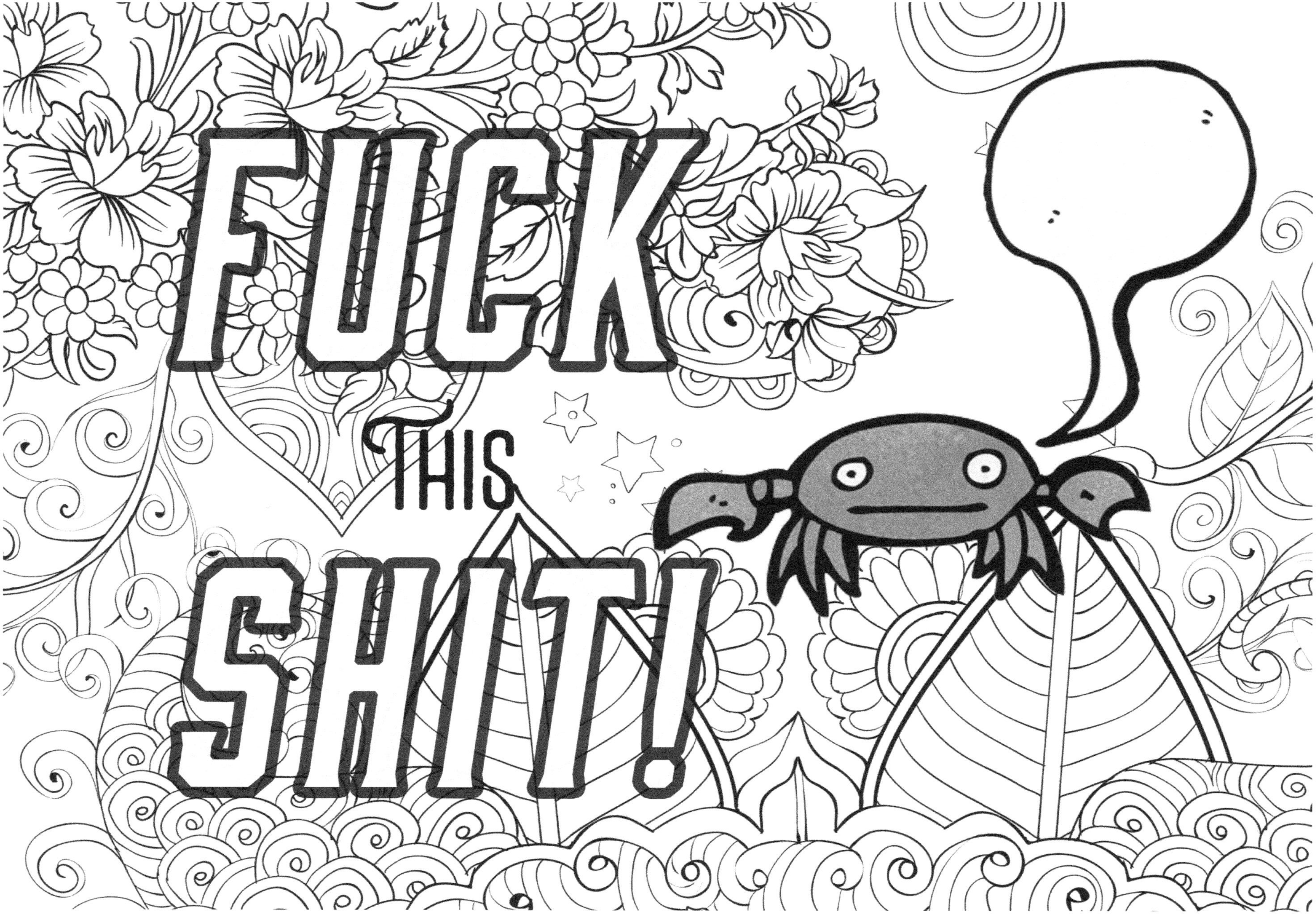
FUCK
THIS
SHIT!

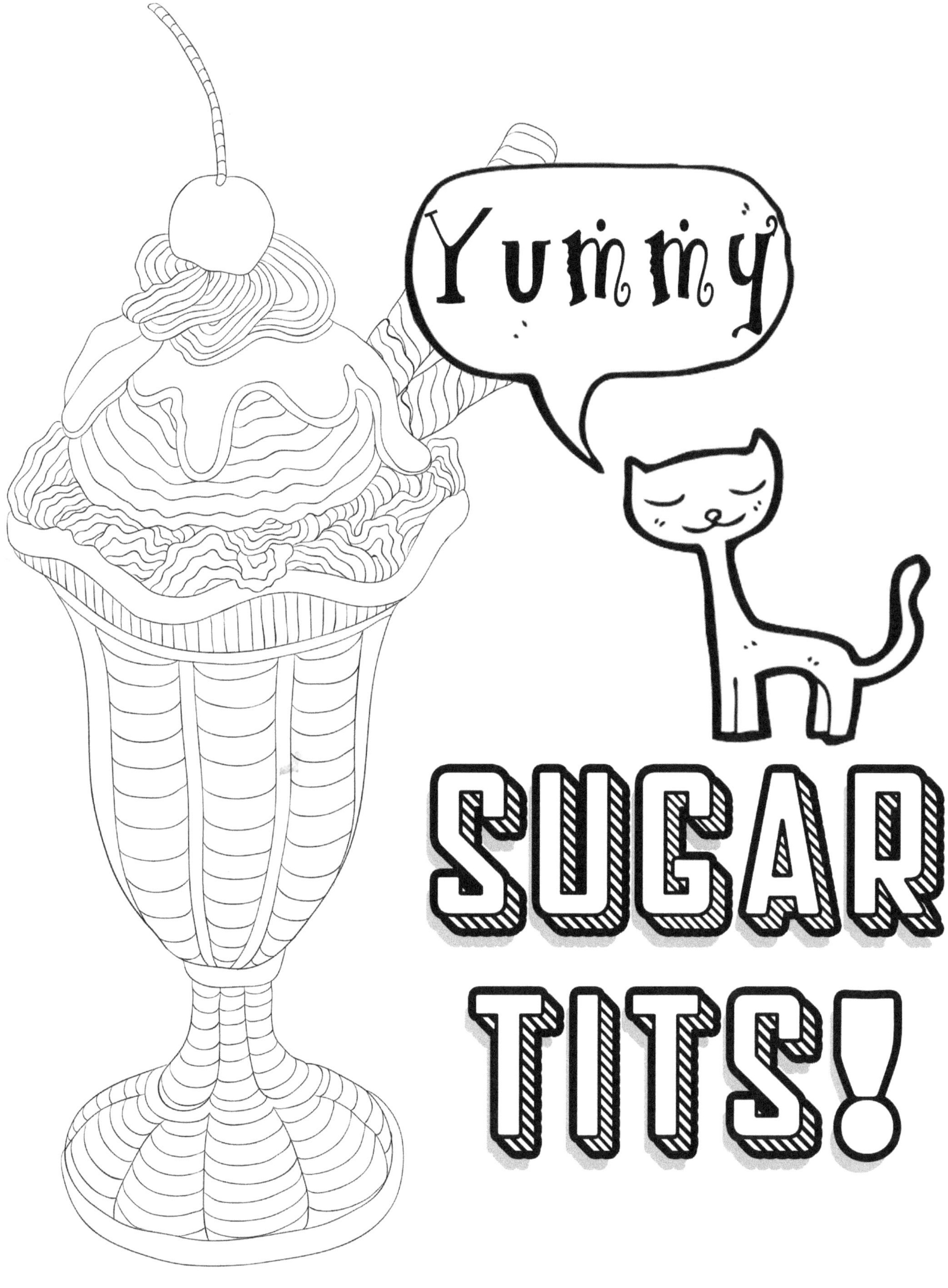
Yummy
SUGAR
TITS!

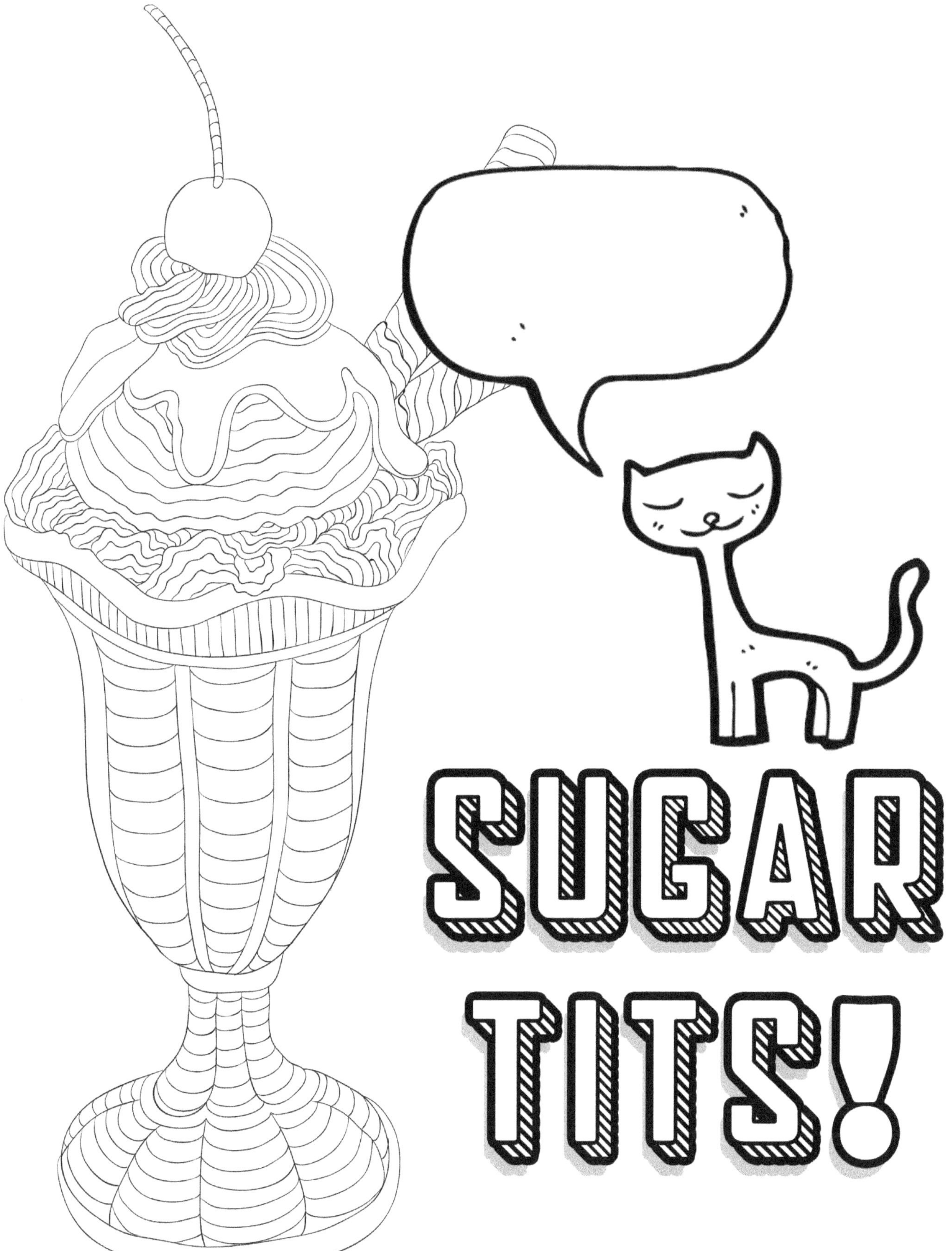
SUGAR
TITS!

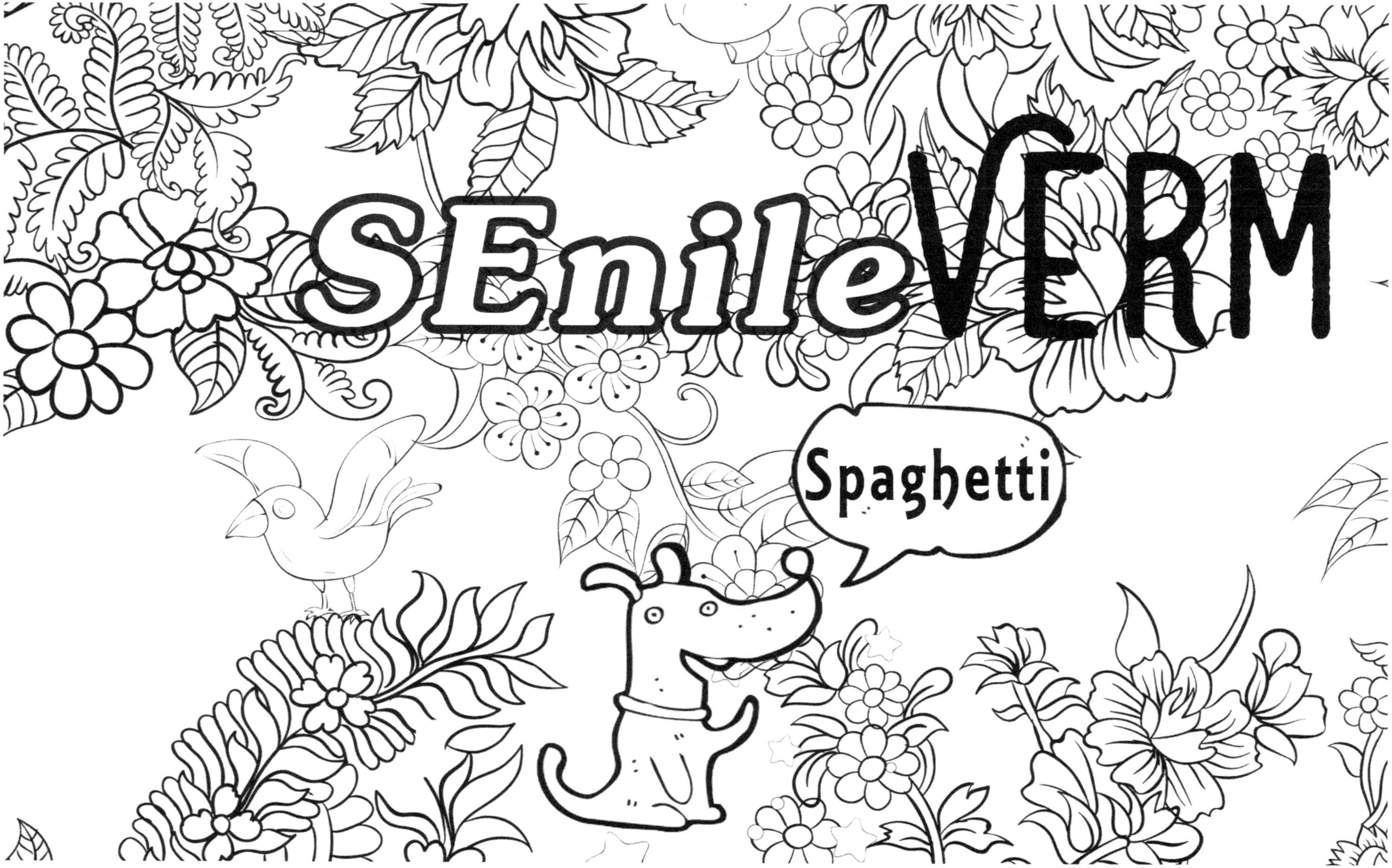
SEnileVERM
Spaghetti

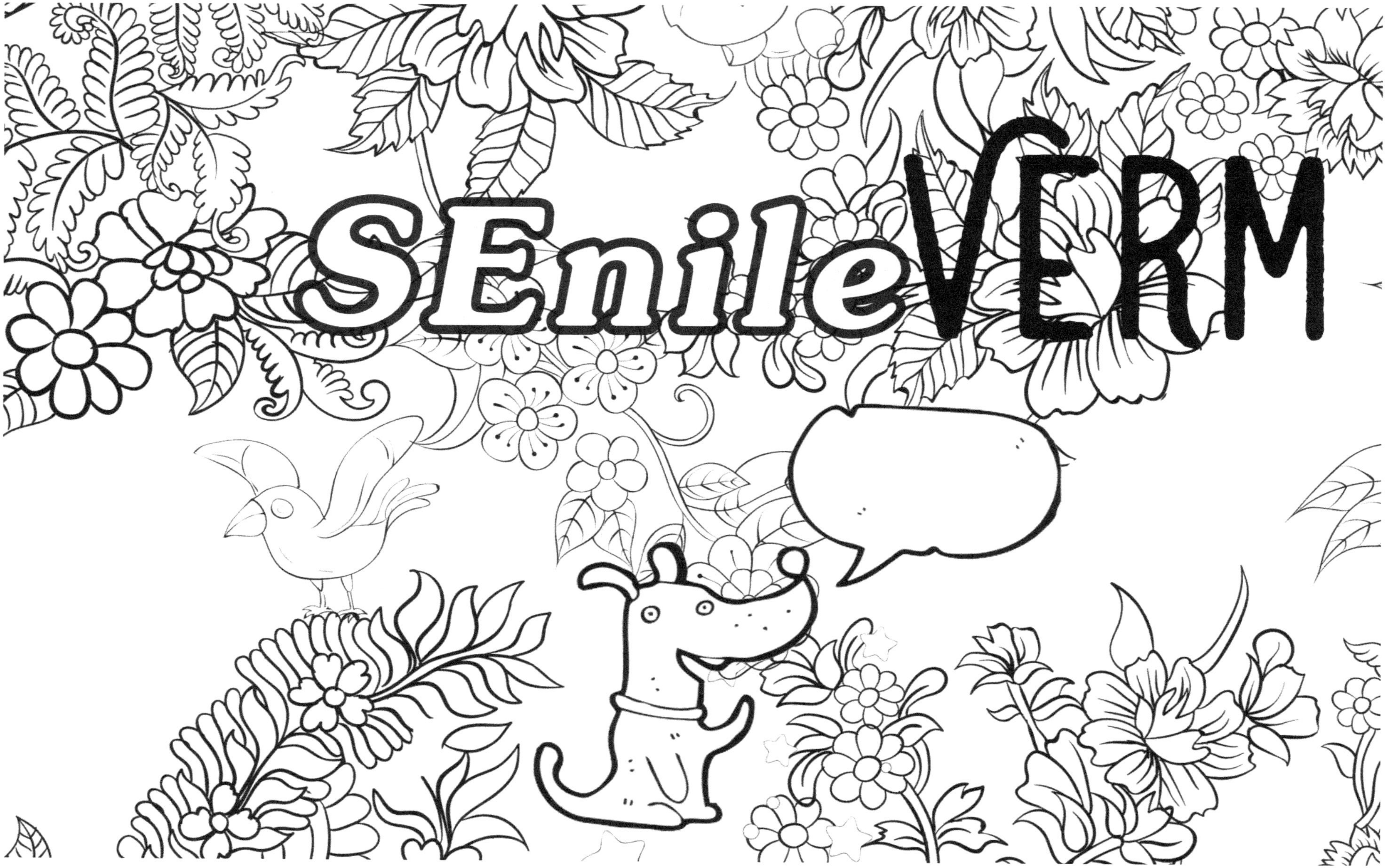
SEnileVERM

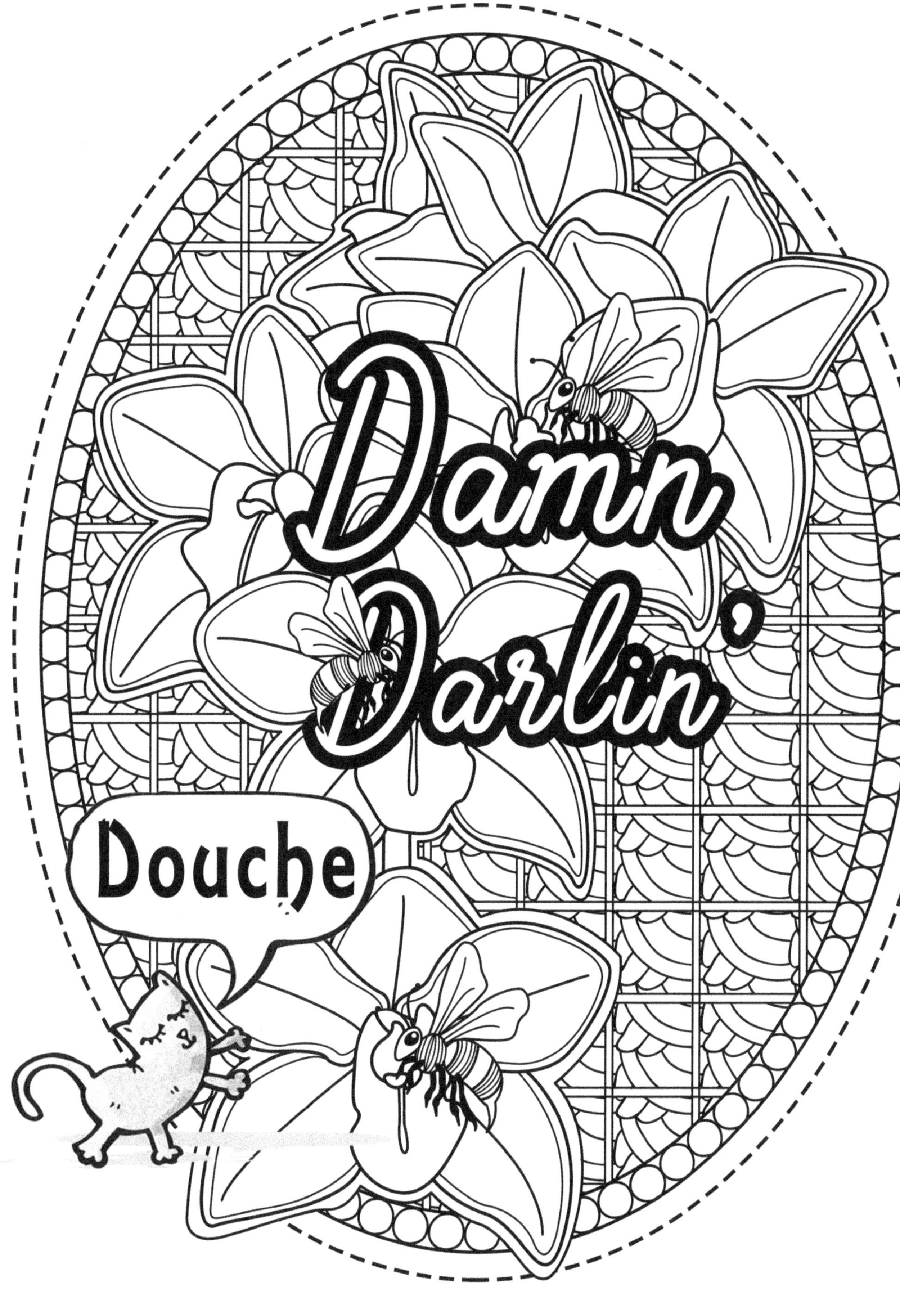
Damn Darlin'
Douche

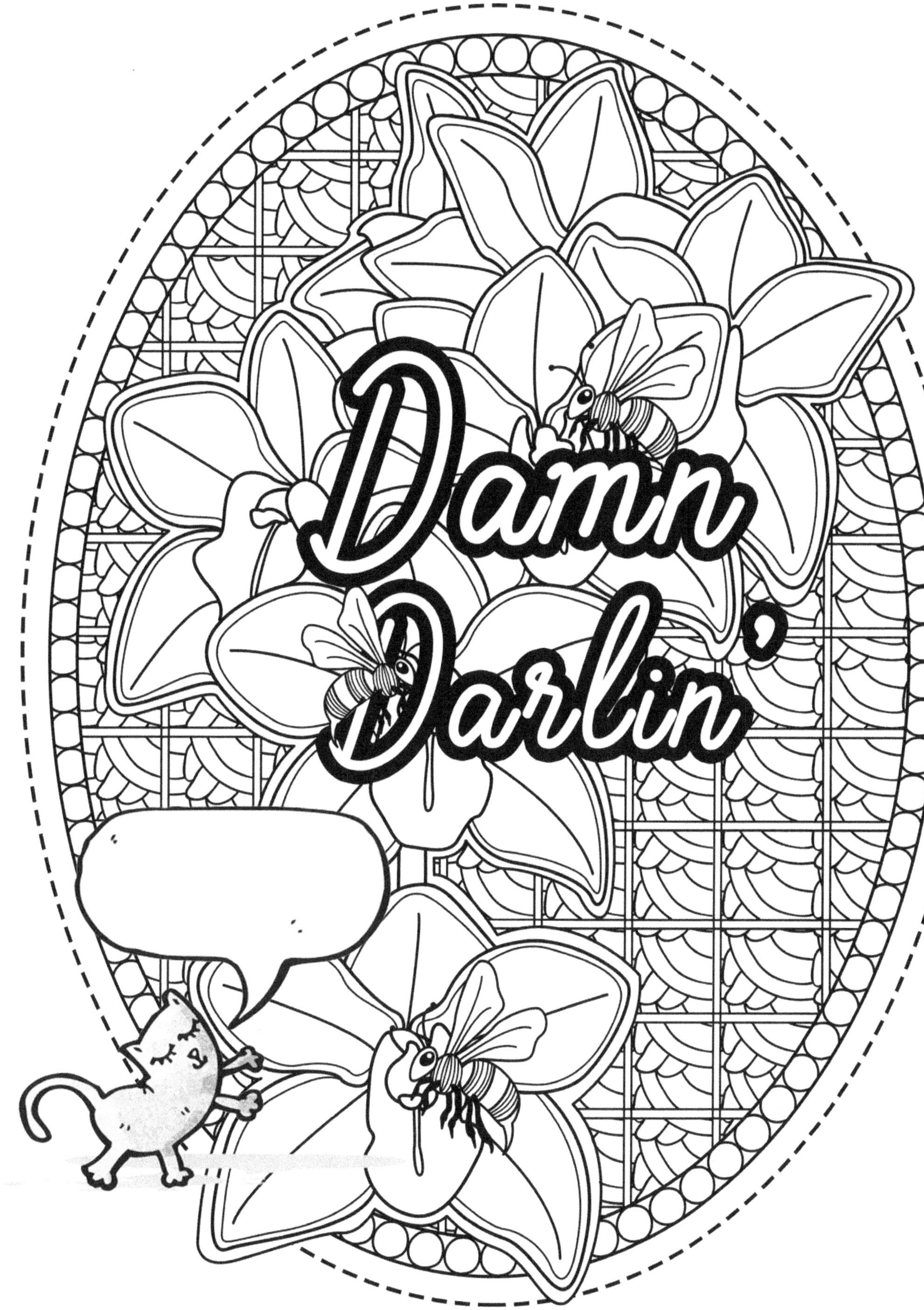
Damn
Darlin'

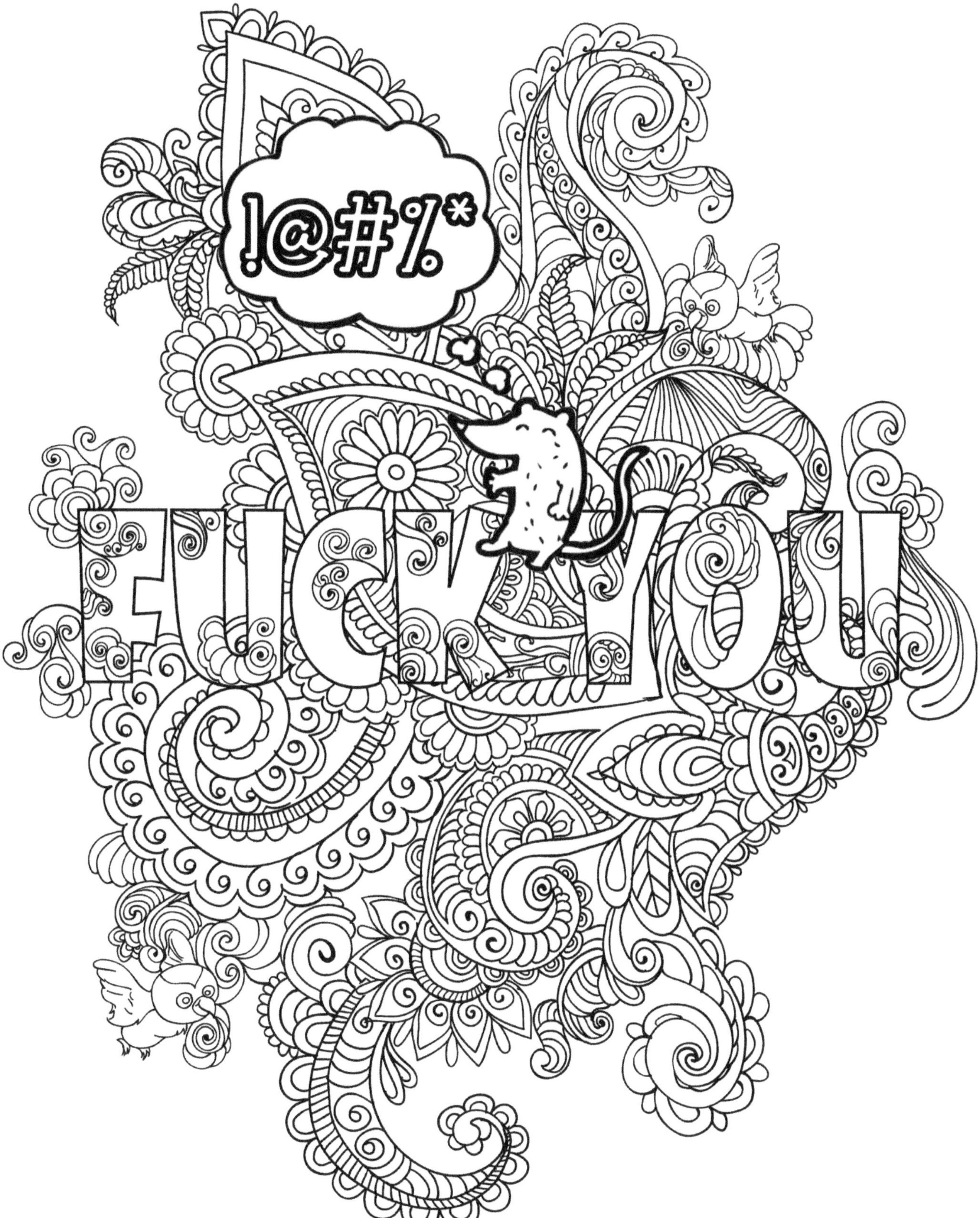
!@#%*
FUCK YOU

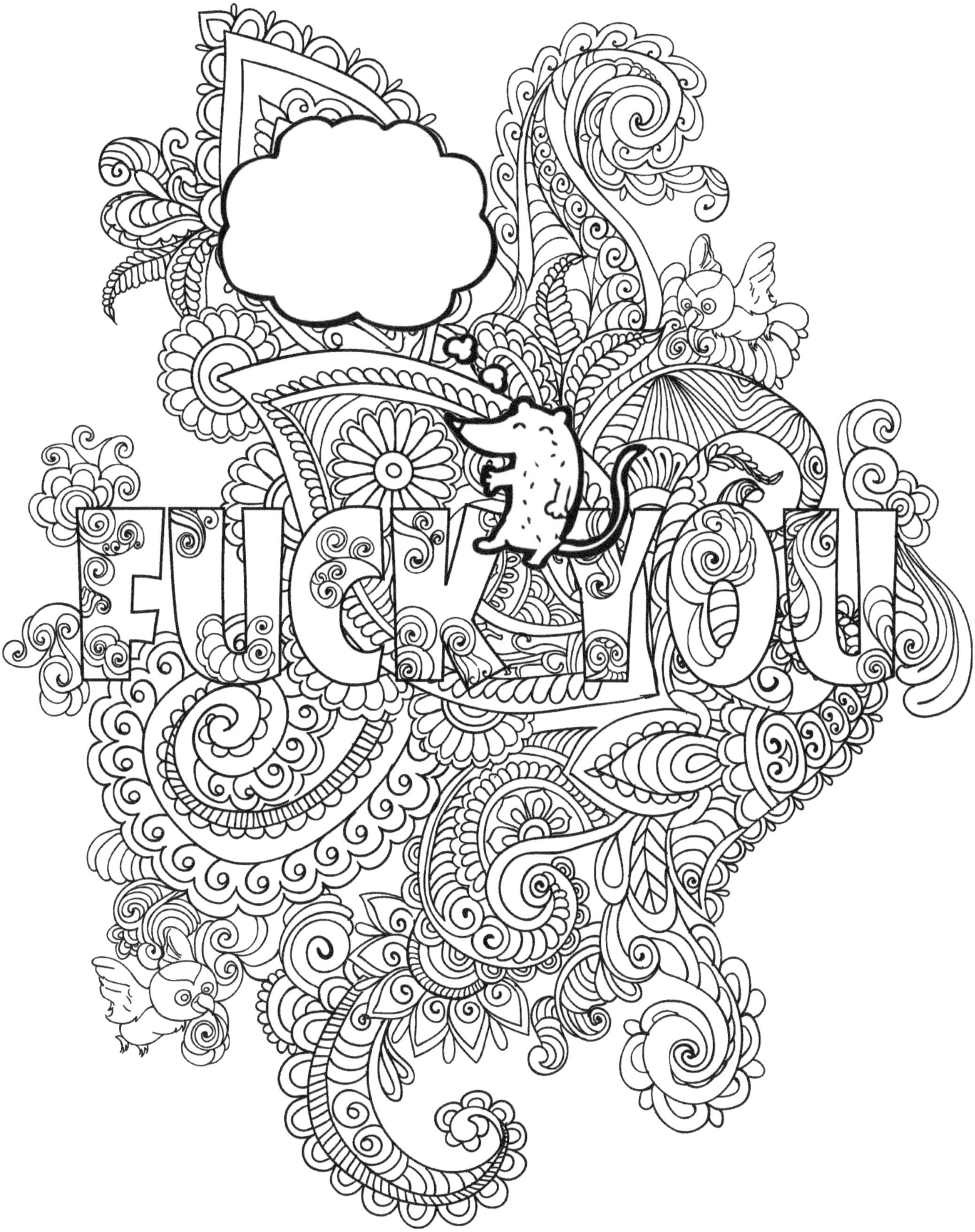
FUCK YOU

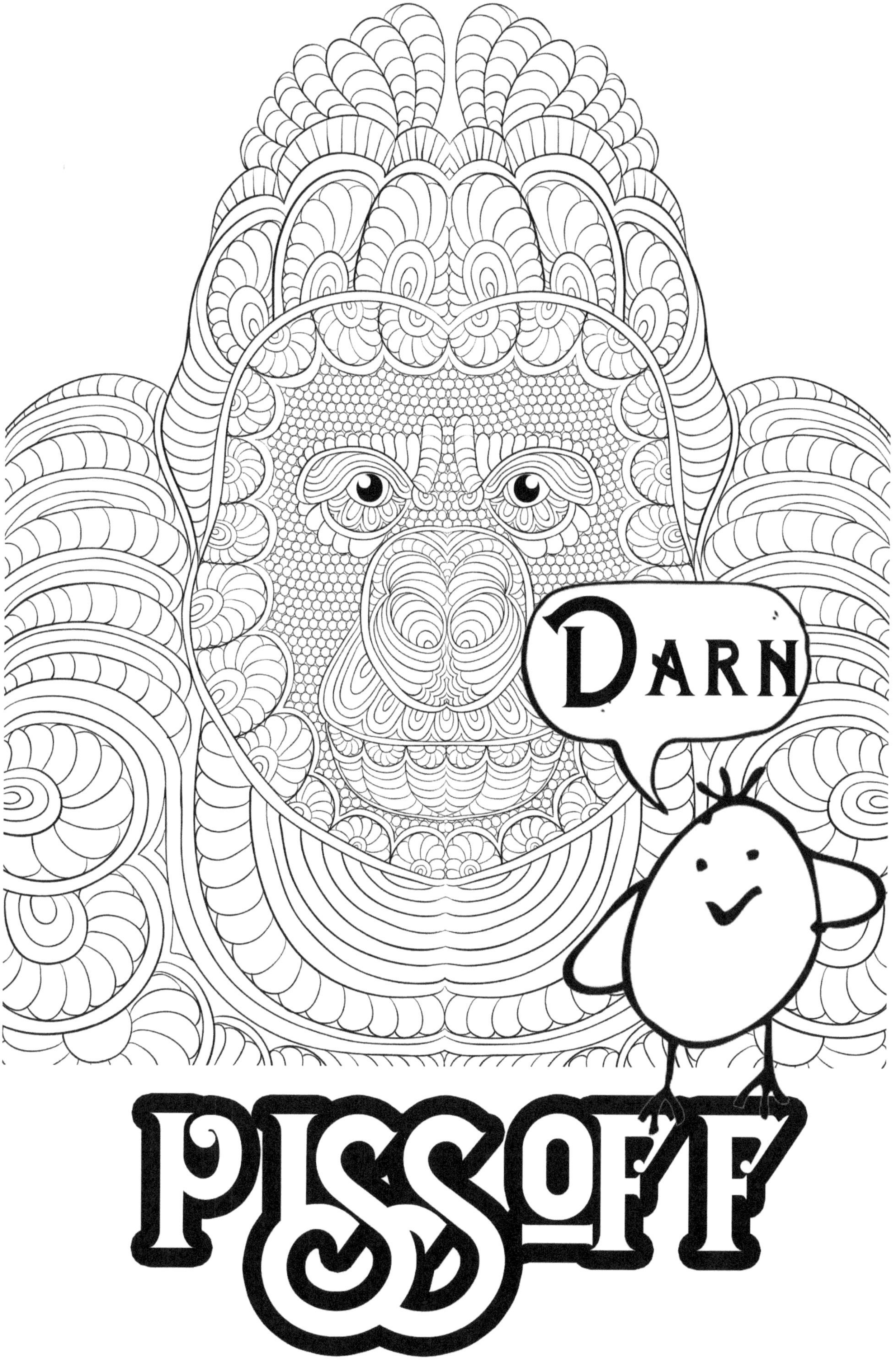
Darn
PISS OFF

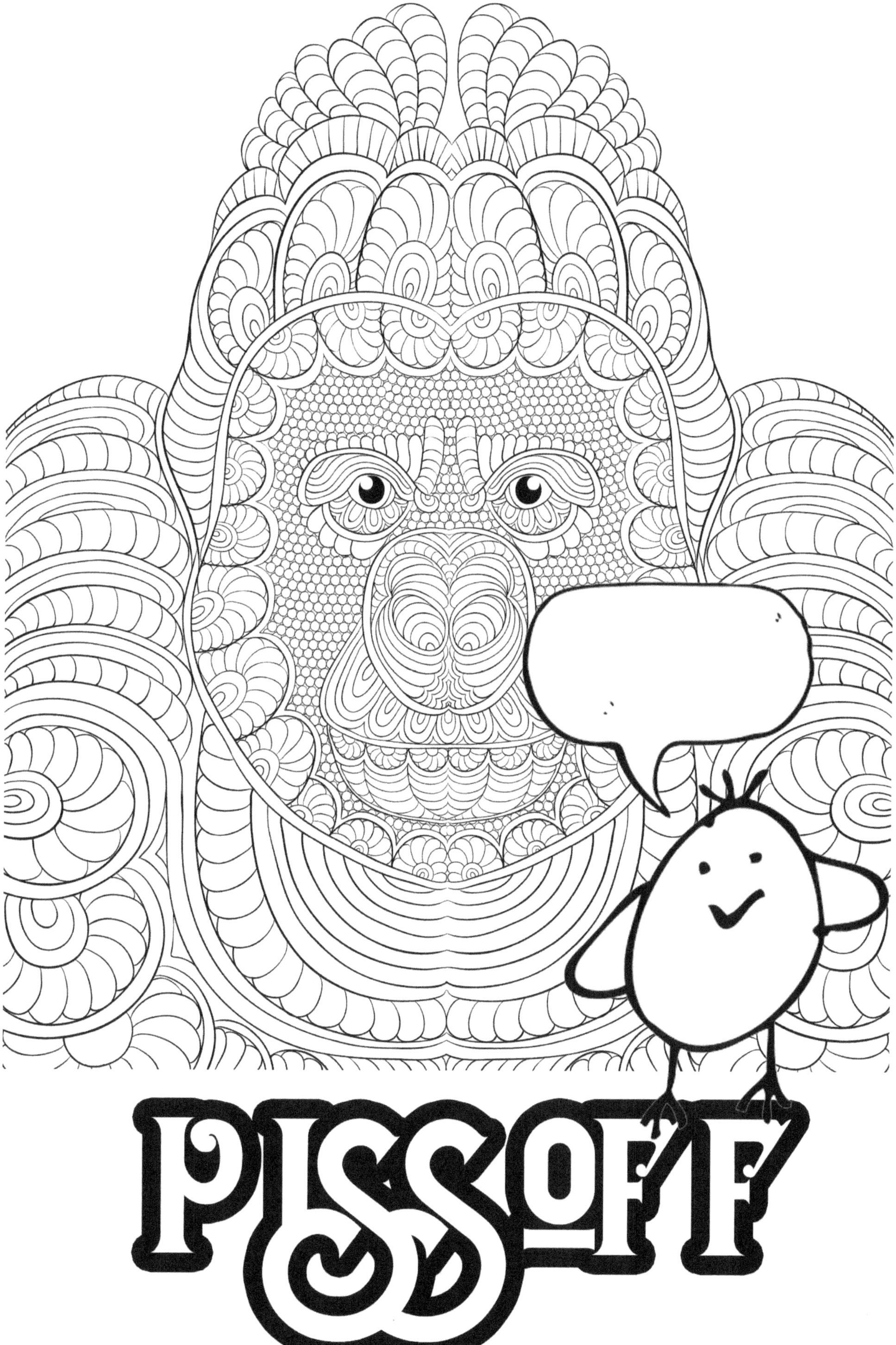
PISS OFF

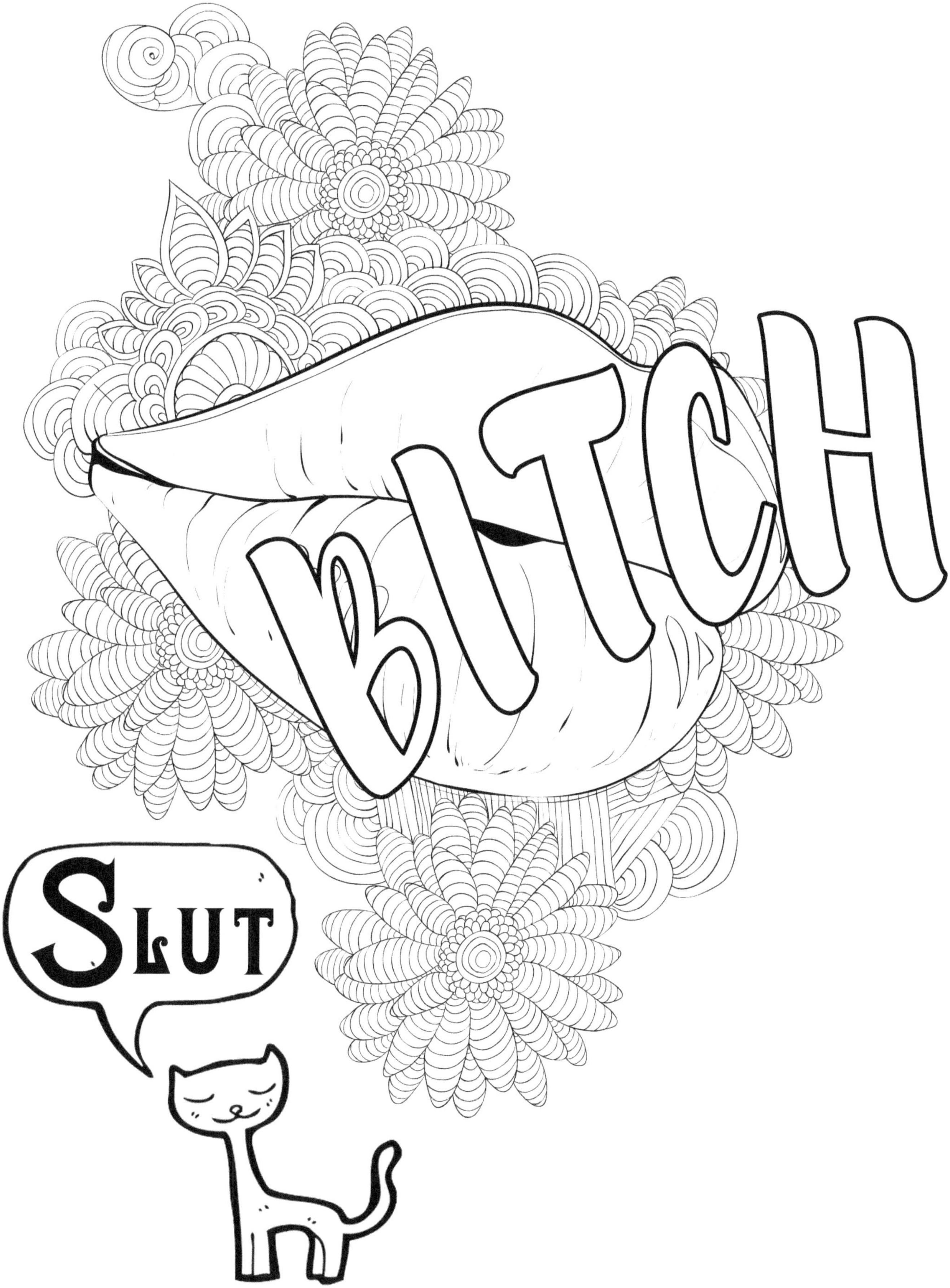
BITCH
SLUT

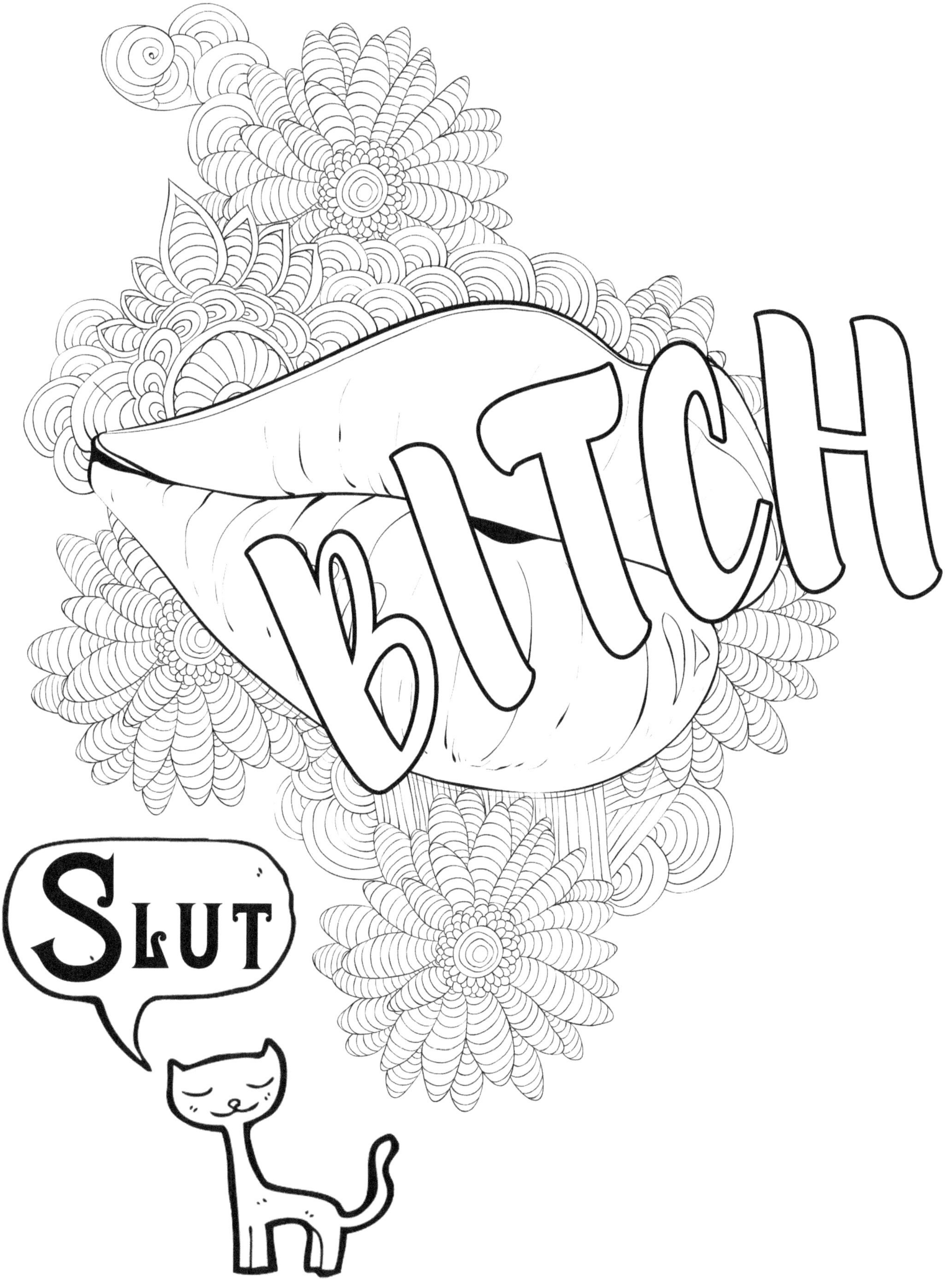
BITCH
SLUT

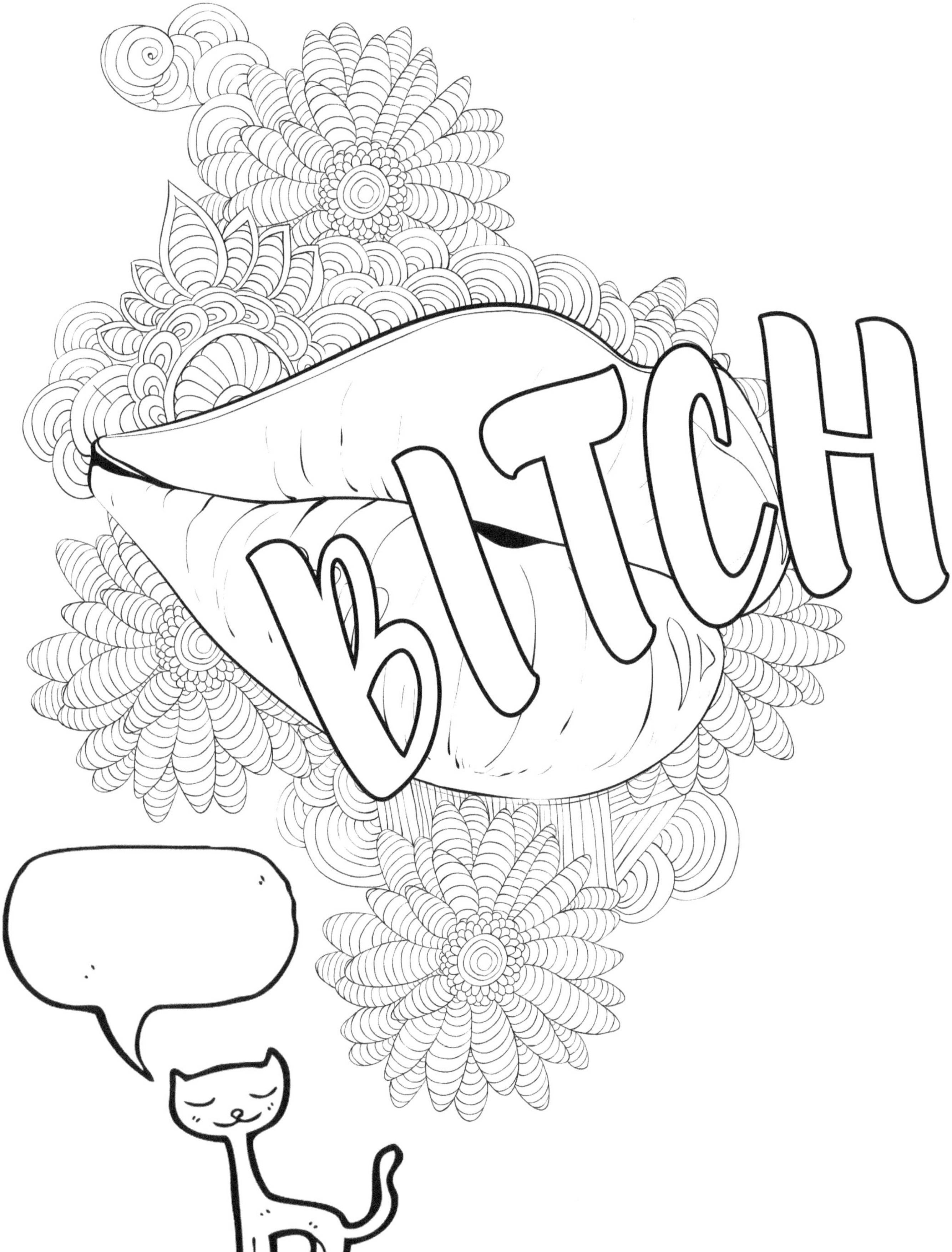
BITCH

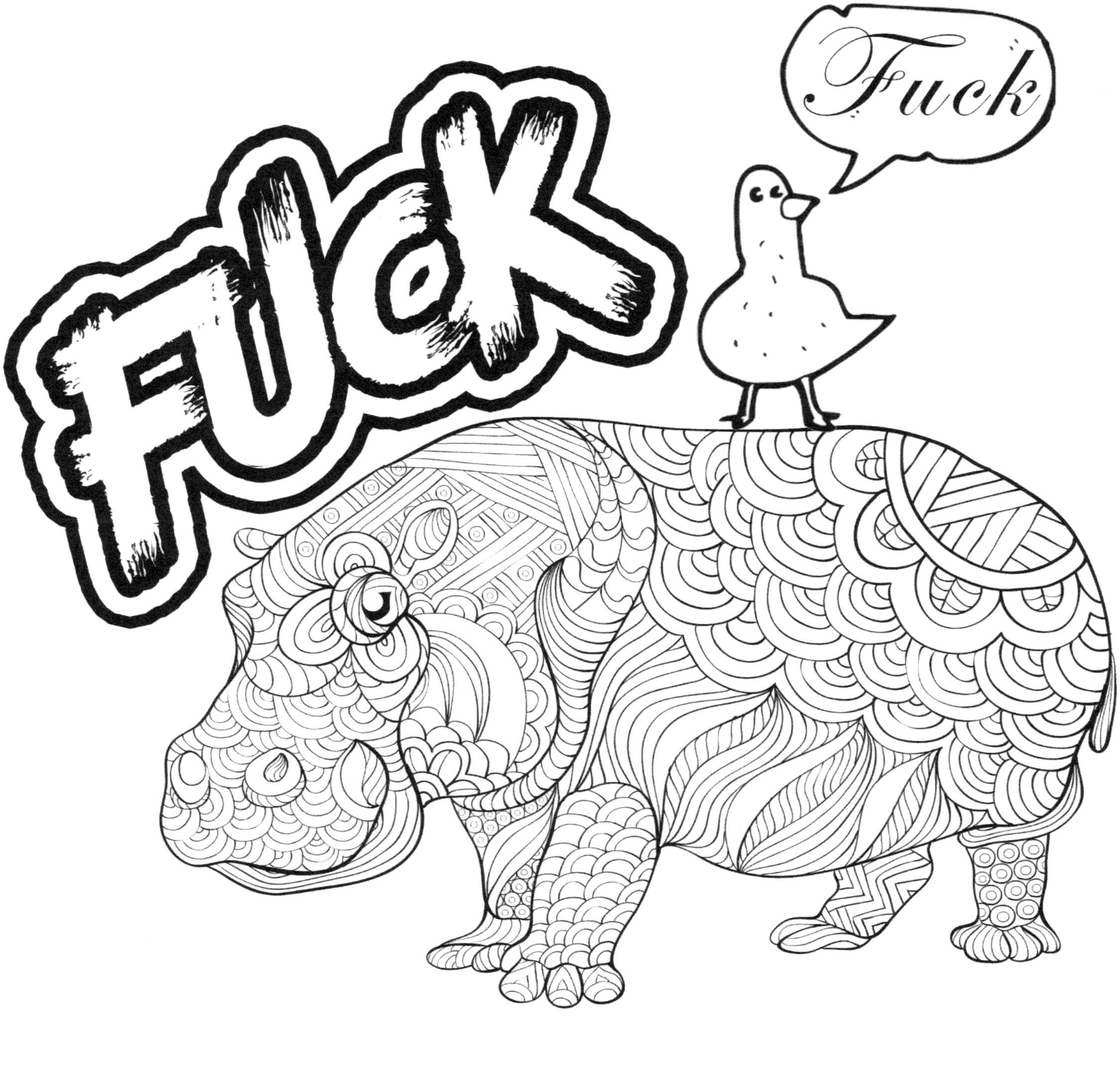
FUCK
Fuck

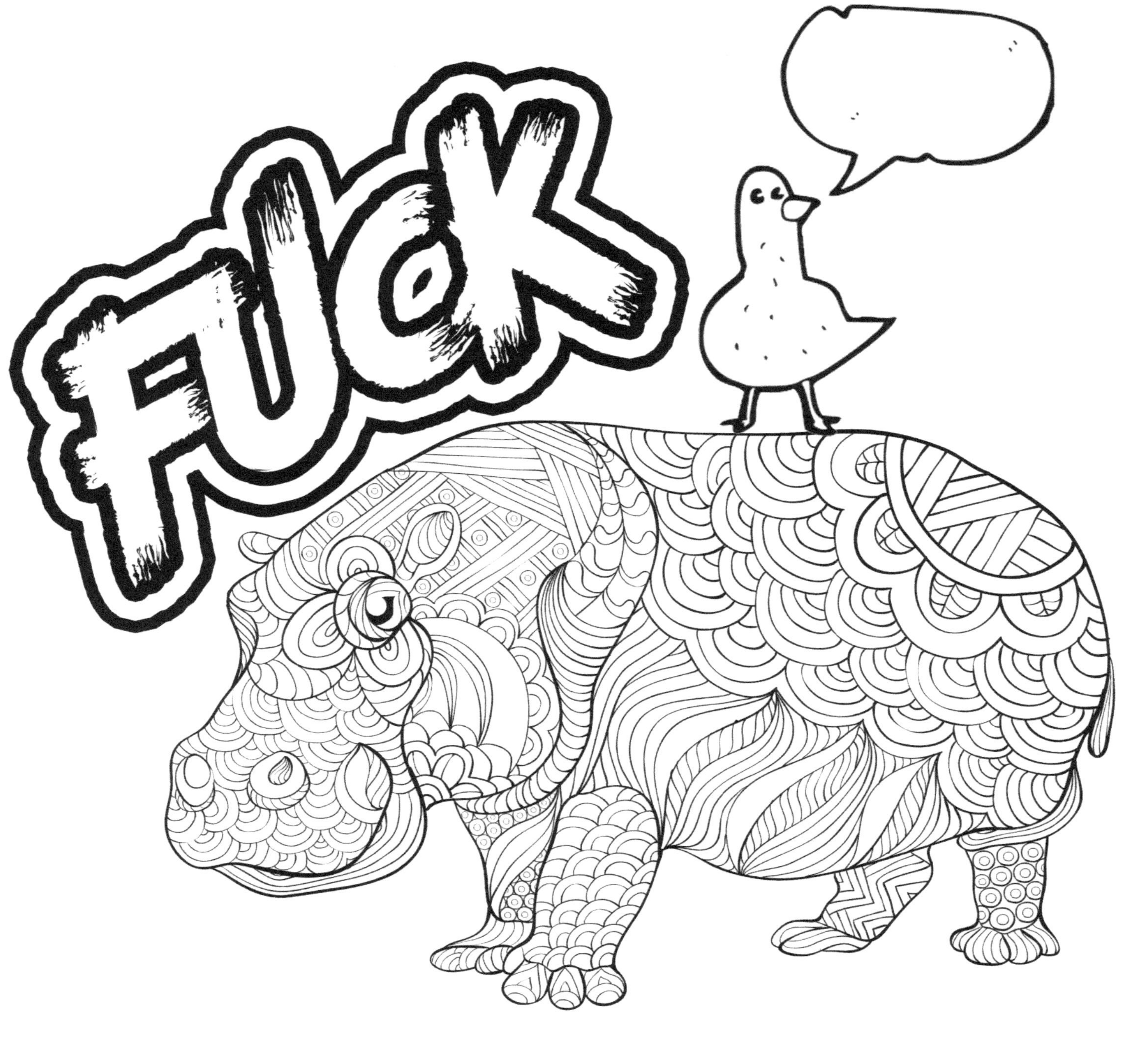
FUCK

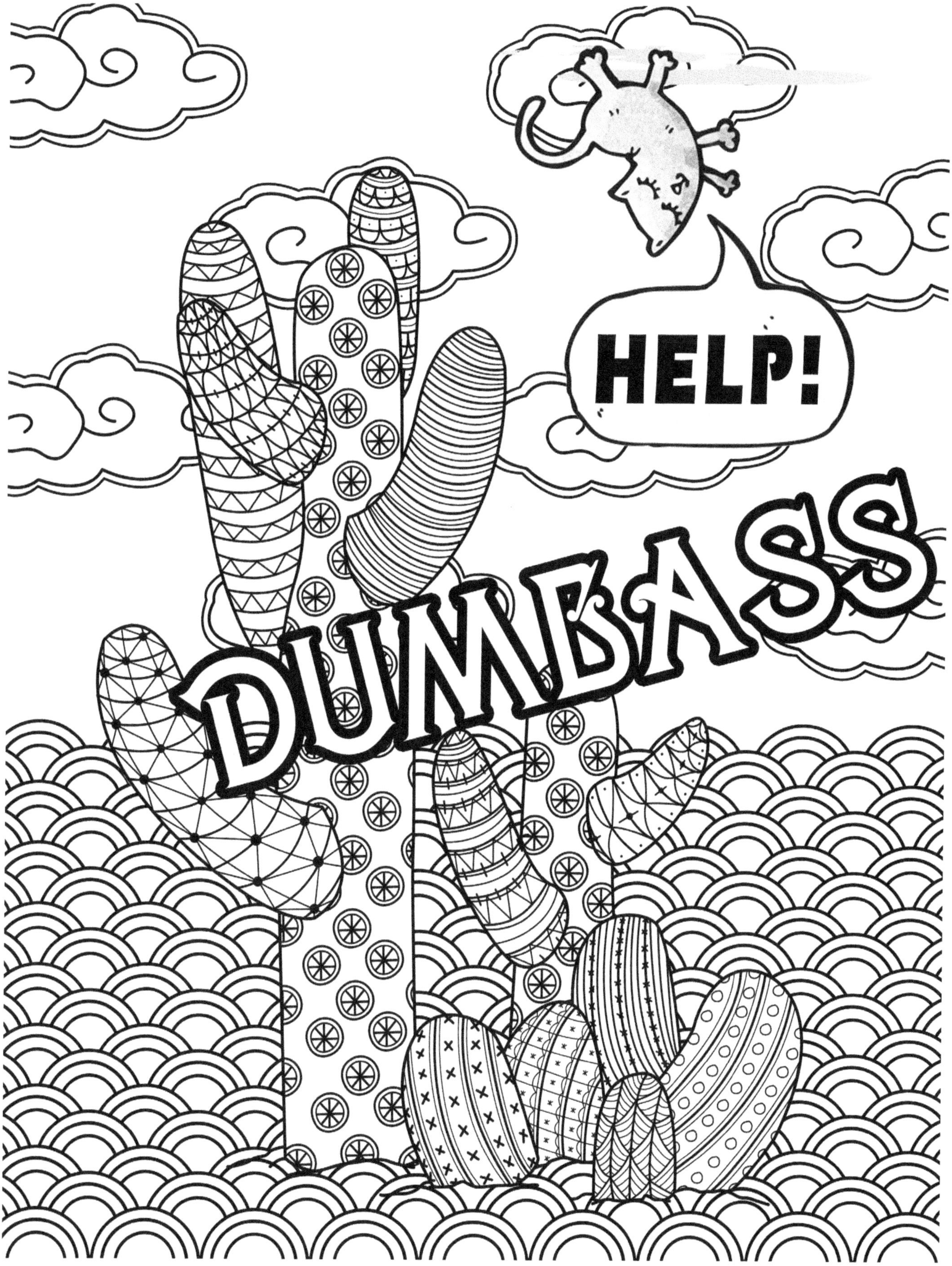
HELP!
DUMBASS

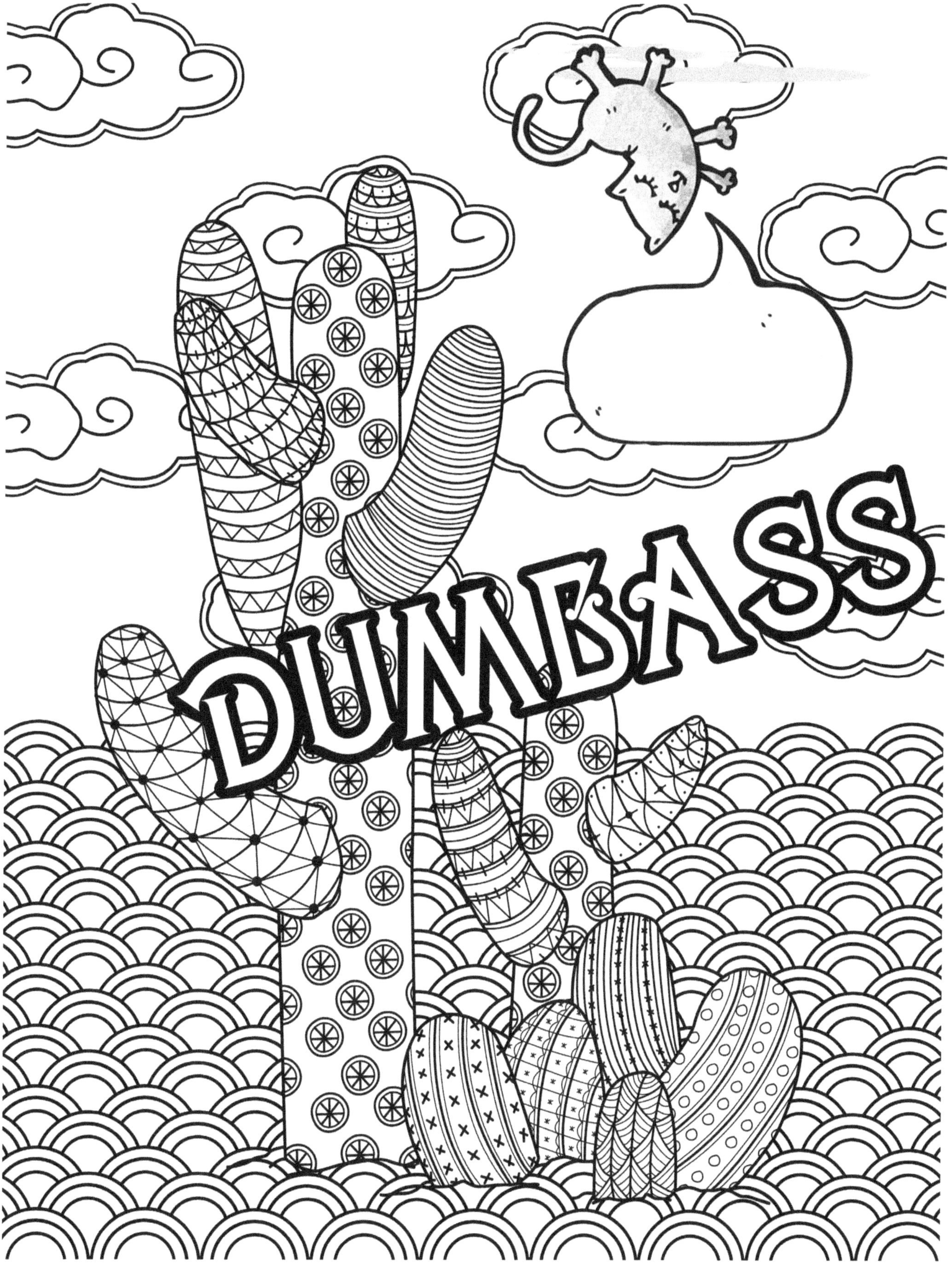
DUMBASS

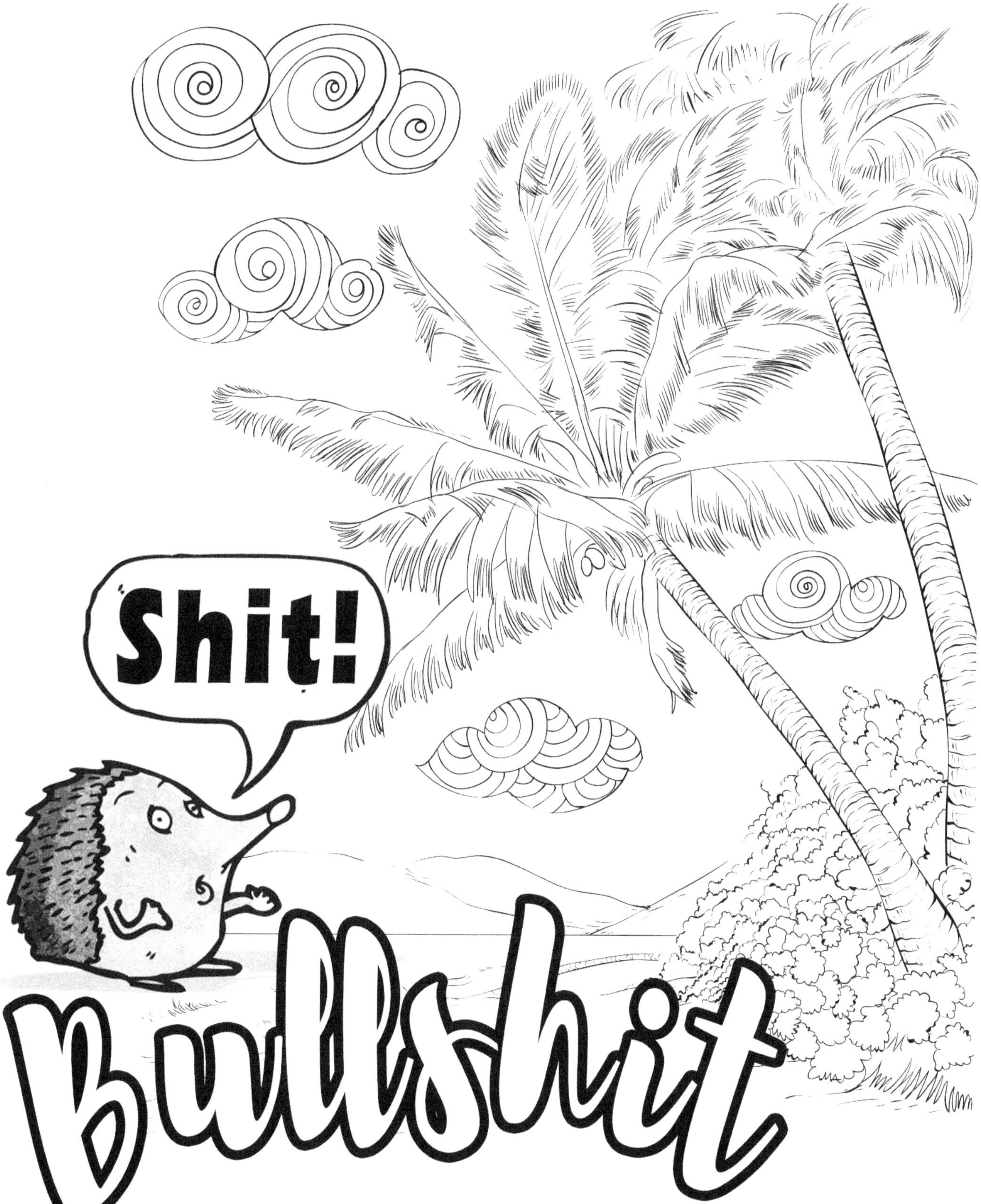
Shit!
Bullshit

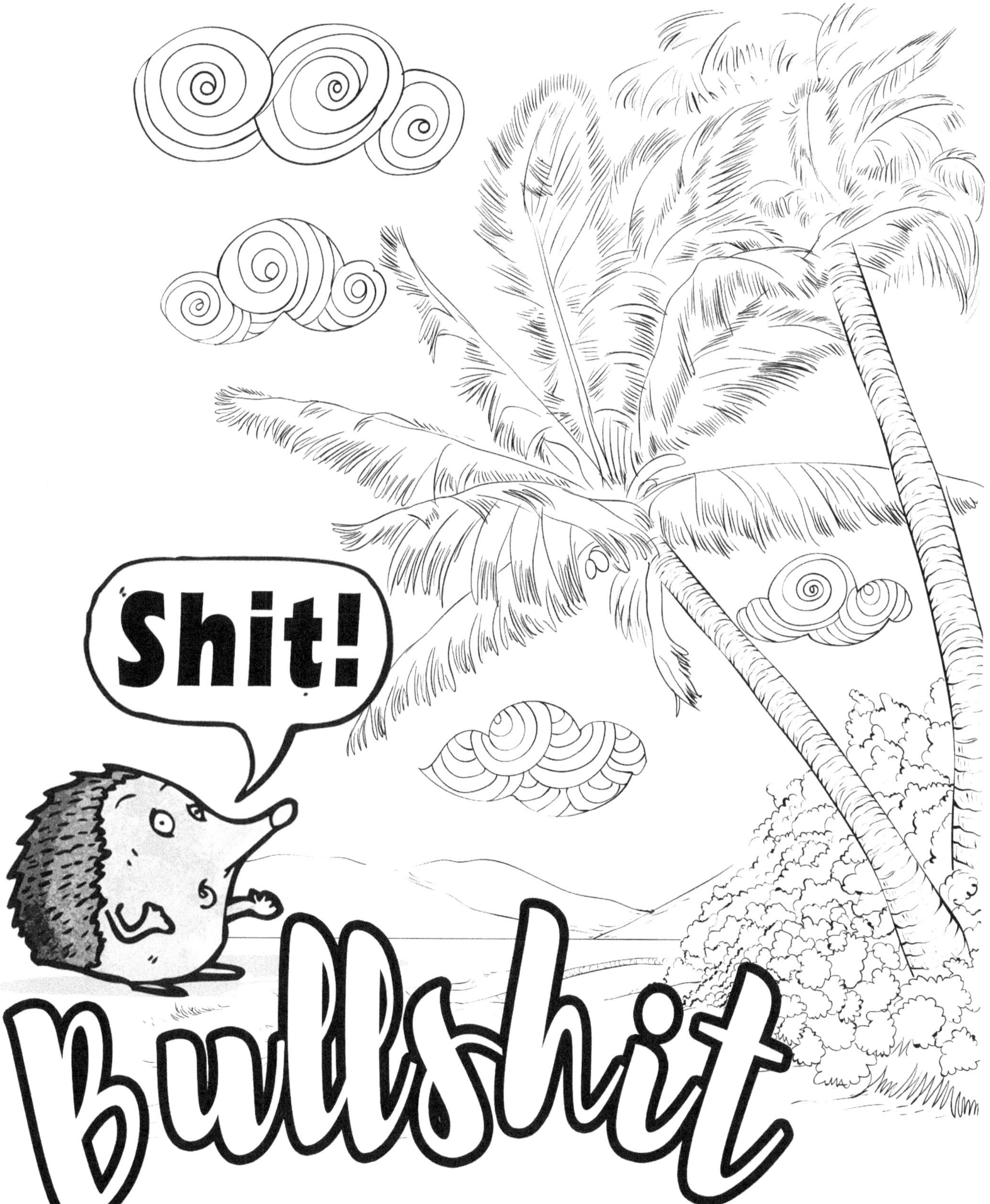
Shit!
Bullshit

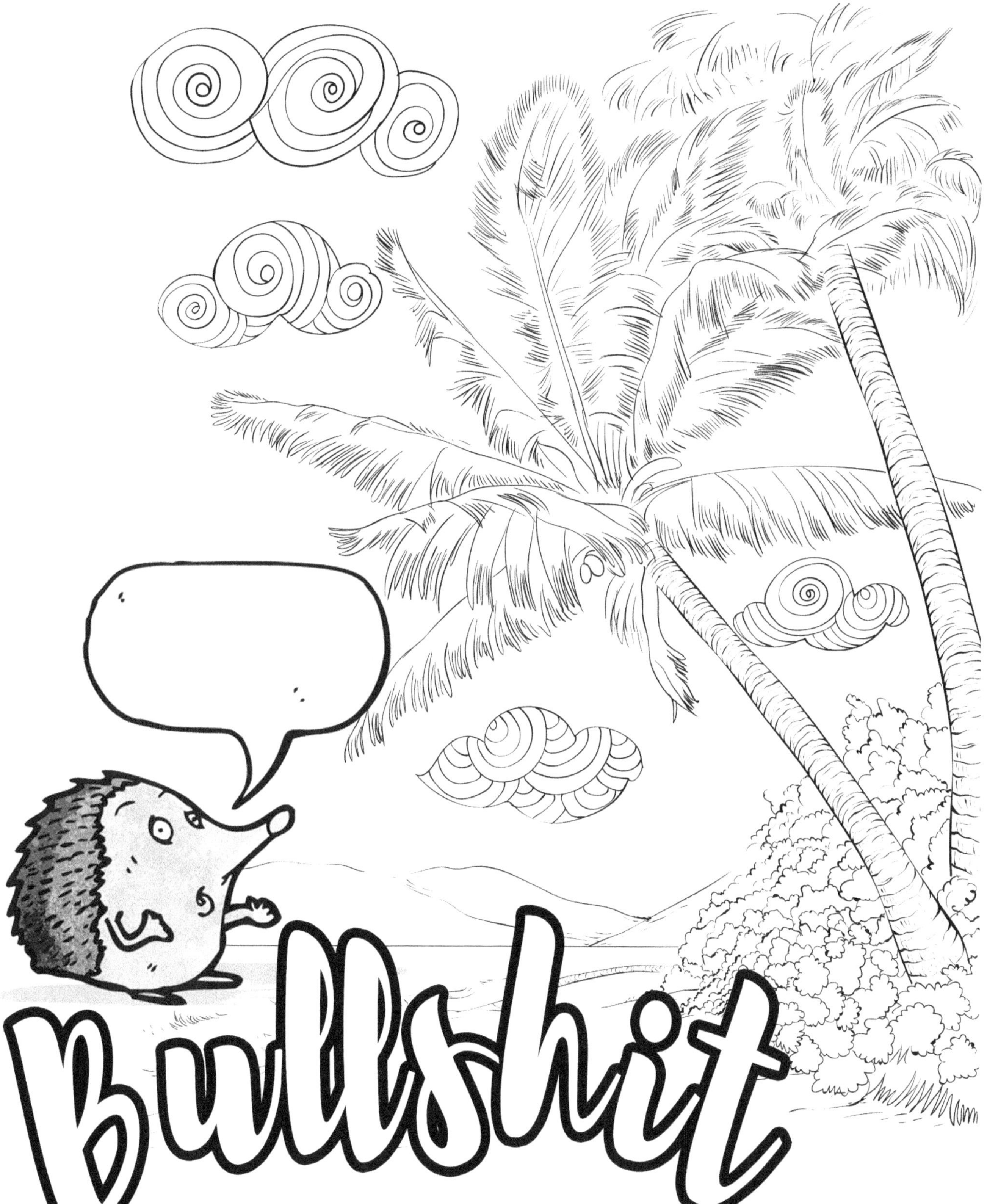
Bullshit

www.ingramcontent.com/pod-product-compliance
Lightning Source LLC
Chambersburg PA
CBHW080624190526
45169CB00009B/3283